VINTAGE CARS

VINTAGE CARS

GENERAL EDITOR: CRAIG CHEETHAM

MOTORBOOKS
INTERNATIONAL

This edition published in 2004 by Motorbooks International, an imprint of MBI
Publishing Company, Galtier Plaza, Suite 200, 380 Jackson Street,
St. Paul, MN 55101-3885 USA

Motorbooks International titles are also available at discounts in bulk quantity for
industrial or sales-promotional use. For details write to Special Sales Manager at
Motorbooks International Wholesalers & Distributors, Galtier Plaza, Suite 200,
380 Jackson Street, St. Paul, MN 55101-3885 USA.

ISBN 0-7603-1873-5

Produced by:
Amber Books Ltd
Bradley's Close
74–77 White Lion Street
London N1 9PF
www.amberbooks.co.uk

Printed in Singapore

CONTENTS

Introduction

When the first Ford Model T rolled off the production line at Dearborn, Michigan in 1906, it was a pivotal moment in motoring history.

Thanks to the forward thinking of one man, motoring grew from being the sole preserve of the rich into transport for the masses. Today, almost a century later, Henry Ford's vision is just as evident as it ever was, with modern high-tech automobile factories employing the same basic manufacturing principles as Ford introduced to the world.

This book celebrates the work of men like Henry Ford—visionary engineers and designers who helped make the motor car the symbol of freedom, status and social emancipation that it has become.

This book looks at cars built from 1910 to the end of World War II—cars that were instrumental in shaping motoring as we know it today, and that were the absolute pinnacle of technological advancement and desirability.

Although their driving characteristics are very different from today's user-friendly motors, these were the finest machines of their day.

The Rolls-Royce Silver Ghost, for example, was capable of speeds of up to 100mph and had legendary reliability—one owner was so impressed with his car that he drove it from England to the Czech Republic and back to demonstrate its durability. Apart from several tyres, three oil changes and a replacement dynamo, the Silver Ghost ran faultlessly throughout the return trip.

Then there were the cars that followed the Model T's rulebook to the letter, bringing motoring to the masses. The Model T's successor, the Model A, was built in four different continents and could be ordered with any body the owner chose, from an open-top sports car to a large delivery van.

At the other end of the scale, there were the untouchables—the cars of film stars and royalty. In America, enormous, flamboyant sedans were the choice of gangsters and movie moguls.

Take the Auburn Speedster. Built to satisfy wealthy customers, the Auburn was extravagantly styled and built to exquisite levels of quality.

But Auburn didn't have the wealthy buyers' market to itself. The Duesenberg Model J and SJ were more than competent rivals, as they too were dripping with bells and whistles that made you feel you'd arrived the moment you got in.

Then there was the Cord. Big, weird-looking, and incredibly spacious, it was a technological tour de force, pioneering such developments as front-wheel-drive and pop-up headlights.

And that was just in the United States. Over in Europe, the Mercedes 540K quickly became recognized as the finest car in Europe. The supercharged roadster had enormous reserves of power and performance that could put many a modern sports car to shame, as well as subtle yet seductive lines.

The Type 35 was one of Bugatti's greatest creations, and among the most beautiful racing cars ever built.

The Spanish Hispano-Suiza was equally beautiful and almost as powerful, while in Italy fabled names such as Alfa Romeo and Lancia were creating luxury cars of their own.

In France, the Delahaye was offering similar levels of luxury to well-heeled motorists, with stunning aerodynamic bodywork and an interior that could only have been inspired by a Paris boutique. Then there was Bugatti. The Royale was perhaps the most extravagant car ever made and holds the record for being the most expensive car ever sold at auction, realizing over $10 million in 1986. But it is sports and racing cars for which Bugatti is best remembered. The nimble Type 35 and aviation-inspired Type 57 are true greats and were instrumental in shaping the sports car legends that would follow.

In Britain, sports cars were also very much the order of the day. The fledgling MG company proved that cars needn't be big nor expensive to deliver true driver pleasure, while fans of more powerful cars could opt for the glorious Invicta S-Type, stylish Lagonda Rapier or race-proven Sunbeam 3-Litre.

With an amazingly refined six-cylinder 7,428 cc engine and advanced four-speed transmission, the Rolls-Royce Silver Ghost was quiet, reliable and very fast for its day.

And who could forget two of the most famous names in British motoring. The Swallow Sidecar SS100, originally built by a motorcycle accessory manufacturer in Blackpool, Lancashire, became the first ever Jaguar—a name synonymous with grace, space and pace.

And then there was Bentley. Multiple winner of the Le Mans 24 Hours race, it became Britain's premium sporting manufacturer with a range of beautiful yet powerful, fine handling cars.

All of these cars and more are gathered here, illustrated with a full set of stunning studio photographs, vivid descriptions and first-hand driving impressions.

Full of evocative and rare machines, this book allows you to step back in time, to a day when motoring was less stressful, cars were objects of art and the technological revolution was at its dawn. Enjoy the ride…

Alfa **ROMEO 6C 1750**

One of the most sought-after Alfa Romeos of all time, the 6C 1750 is a six-cylinder, twin cam designed by Vittorio Jano. Driven by greats like Tazio Nuvolari, it enjoyed success in the classic Mille Miglia race.

"...acceleration is fierce."

"It's surprising how easy the supercharged Alfa is to drive. Light and equally positive high-geared steering means the car can be placed absolutely precisely. Despite the non-synchromesh, the close-ratio transmission is easy to use, and has a light clutch. Even when left in top gear acceleration is impressive—the supercharger gives the impression the engine ahead of you in the cockpit is much greater than a mere 1.75 liters in size."

A very upright driving position characterizes the legendary Alfa 1750.

Milestones

1929 Alfa improves
the 6C 1500 by increasing the displacement of the twin-cam six. Racing success comes right away. Campari and Ramponi win the Mille Miglia at an average speed of 56 mph, and another car wins the Spa 24 Hours in Belgium.

All 1750s were coachbuilt by outside companies.

1930 It's a repeat
performance for the 1750, as the new Gran Sport version with its larger supercharger wins the Mille Miglia, with the great Tazio Nuvolari driving.

This 1929 Supersport is a tuned version of the 1750.

1931 The 1750 GTC
Sports sedan arrives, built on a long-wheelbase chassis.

1933 The 1750 is
replaced by the eight-cylinder 8C 2300 series.

UNDER THE SKIN

Steel boxed-section chassis

Live rear axle

Leaf-sprung suspension

Cast-iron in-line-six

Strong tradition

The chassis design on the 6C 1750 is quite straightforward, with two deep box-section framerails running lengthwise. These kick up at the rear to clear the live axle and arch slightly at the front to make room for the beam front axle. They are connected longitudinally by three main crossmembers. The suspension is similar to the setup found on most contemporary cars; it has a solid-beam front axle and semi-elliptic leaf springs.

THE POWER PACK

Ahead of its time

Although Alfa now has a huge reputation for its alloy engines, the 6C 1750's power plant is made from cast-iron except for an alloy crankcase and oil pan for better cooling. It is an in-line, six-cylinder engine with a long stroke and a very advanced specification: two overhead camshafts driven by a vertical shaft at the back of the engine with bevel gears. They open two valves per cylinder, angled at 90 degrees to each other to give a very efficient crossflow-type combustion chamber. There is a single spark plug per cylinder mounted vertically between the valves. Power ranges from 45 bhp up to 102 bhp in supercharged, fixed head racing form.

Open sport

All 6C 1750s are highly prized today, but if there is a pick of the range, it is perhaps one of the swoopy convertibles that were either bodied by Zagato or Touring. In Super sport or Gran sport form, they usually have very powerful supercharged engines.

Sleekest of the 6C 1750s are the open-top models.

Alfa ROMEO 6C 1750

There are some ordinary, even dull-looking 1750s, but the convertibles by Zagato, Touring, and Castagna are among the most perfectly styled and proportioned sports cars ever made.

Supercharger

The 1750's twin-cam layout guarantees power, but for real performance Alfa added a Roots-type supercharger. This is driven off the crankshaft at the front of the engine.

Separate chassis

There was much more development in engines than in the chassis in the 1930s, so the 1750's basic boxed-section chassis is little changed from that found on the earlier 1500.

Twin-cam engine

This 1.75-liter, in-line six is the engine that really started Alfa's great twin-cam reputation.

Four-speed transmission

All 1750s have a four-speed transmission mounted in line with the engine. Early cars have crash boxes, but from the sixth series cars of 1933, there is synchromesh on third and fourth gears.

Live rear axle

Independent rear suspension was not a viable option in the late 1920s, so there is a live rear axle held and located by semi-elliptic leaf springs.

Specifications
1932 Alfa Romeo 6C 1750 Super Sport

ENGINE

Type: In-line six cylinder
Construction: Cast-iron block and head, with alloy crankcase and sump
Valve gear: Two valves per cylinder operated by double gear-driven overhead camshafts via adjustable tappets
Bore and stroke: 2.56 in. x 3.46 in.
Displacement: 1,752 cc
Compression ratio: 5.0:1
Induction system: Single Memini carburetor with mechanical Roots-type supercharger
Maximum power: 85 bhp at 4,500 rpm
Maximum torque: N/A
Top speed: 95 mph
0–60 mph: 14.0 sec.

TRANSMISSION

Four-speed manual

BODY/CHASSIS

Separate steel channel-section chassis frame with choice of coachbuilt bodywork

SPECIAL FEATURES

A rumble seat is used to carry additional passengers.

The windshield can be folded forward for competition use.

RUNNING GEAR

Steering: Worm-and-wheel
Front suspension: Beam axle with semi-elliptic leaf springs and adjustable friction shock absorbers
Rear suspension: Live axle with torque tube, semi-elliptic leaf springs, and adjustable friction shock absorbers
Brakes: Finned alloy drums, 12.6-in. dia.
Wheels: Rudge Whitworth center fixing knock-on/off wire spoke, 18-in. dia.
Tires: 5.00 x 18

DIMENSIONS

Length: 156.0 in. **Width:** 65.0 in.
Height: 55.6 in. **Wheelbase:** 108.0 in.
Track: 54.3 in. (front and rear)
Weight: 2,072 lbs.

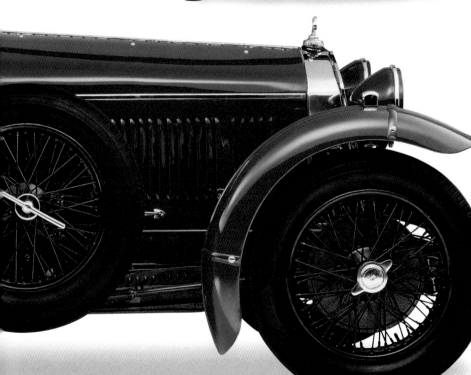

Alfa **ROMEO 8C 2300**

In the depths of the Depression in the 1930s Alfa was brave enough to introduce an expensive sports racer. The 8C 2300 was an instant winner, dominating Le Mans and the Mille Miglia.

...send the revs soaring."

"You'll be astonished at the engine's response to the slightest touch of the throttle which really winds up the engine. Unusually, the throttle is in between the brake and clutch. The steering is extremely direct and the springing hard, making the Alfa instantly responsive with beautifully balanced handling. The Alfa responds better the faster it is driven. As the steering lightens, the 2300 becomes more neutral and easy to balance on the throttle. The huge brakes stop the car on a dime with change to spare."

Stylish and functional, the 8C 2300's dashboard layout is simple and effective. However, tall drivers may find their legs wedged under that large steering wheel.

Milestones

1931 Alfa Romeo chooses the mille Miglia as the race in which to give the 8C 2300 its debut, but both cars crash. Alfa makes no mistake in the Targa Florio, with Tazio Nuvolari winning. This victory is followed by a win in the Italian GP. The 8C 2300 also wins the 24 hours of Le Mans.

Legendary Tazio Nuvolari won the 1933 Mille Miglia in an 8C 2300.

1932 Another Le Mans win for the 8C 2300. The Mille Miglia also falls to the Alfa.

Although different chassis lengths were available, most carried sporty two-seater bodywork.

1933 Alfa wins again at Le Mans with Nuvolari/Sommer finishing just 10 seconds ahead of the next 8C 2300. The agile Alfa is on a winning streak and claims victory again at the Mille Miglia.

1934 8C 2300's dominance continues with another Le Mans win and Mille Miglia victory. Production ends but the cars keep winning.

UNDER THE SKIN

Chassis choice

The Alfa's traditional ladder frame chassis meant it could easily be built with three different wheelbases depending on bodywork carried, the racing Monza models having the shortest wheelbase. All versions have live rear axles with semi-elliptic springs and twin friction shocks. The solid front axle is also mounted on semi-elliptic springs. Large drum brakes are used all around.

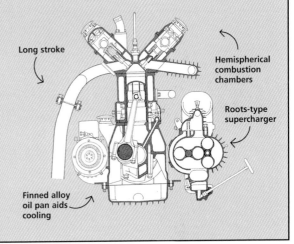

Choice of chassis lengths

Leaf-sprung live rear axle

Separate ladder frame chassis

Solid front axle

Bi-block, in-line eight

THE POWER PACK

Great eight

Alfa's eight-cylinder, all-alloy 2.3-liter twin cam has the camshaft drive in the center of the engine between the two engine blocks to reduce the stress on the long cams. The engine can almost be regarded as two four-cylinder blocks joined together. It is a tall, undersquare unit with a long stroke and uses a supercharger driven from the crank to pressurize the single carburetor. It was designed by Vittorio Jano, one of the greatest pre-war engine designers.

Long stroke

Hemispherical combustion chambers

Roots-type supercharger

Finned alloy oil pan aids cooling

Mighty Monza

Quickest of all the 8C 2300 variants was the Monza, built on the shortest chassis and was a Mille Miglia winner in 1934 as well as a GP racer. It was stripped of lights and mudguards. From 1932 it could be built in single-seater form.

The stripped-out Monza was a successful road and circuit racer.

Alfa ROMEO 8C 2300

The 8C 2300 was a masterpiece by one of Alfa Romeo's greatest designers, Vittorio Jano. In the early 1930s there was nothing to match its supercharged performance on Europe's great road races.

Twin-cam engine

The Alfa needed a long hood to house the alloy straight-eight engine with its two gear-driven overhead camshafts, which gave an excellent 142 bhp at 5,200 rpm.

Cutaway doors

Doors on cars such as the Alfa were cut away because drivers needed the room for their elbows when steering and higher doors would have got in the way in such narrow cockpits.

Hood straps

The hood has conventional latches but many of the roads on which the Alfas raced were rough and bumpy and straps avoided the chance of the hood flying open at high speed.

Knock-on wheels

Punctures were common in the Alfa's day and the wire wheels were designed to be changed very quickly. The big center nut could be knocked on or off quickly with a soft hammer to release the wheel.

Tool box

The battery box on one side was mirrored by the tool box on the other. Tools were a must as cars of this era needed constant maintenance and adjustment.

Quick release fuel filler

Quick release fuel caps were used so race mechanics could flip them open immediately and pour fuel in from large drums.

Fold-flat windshield

For racing the windshield could be folded flat, slightly reducing the frontal area of the car and thus increasing its speed.

Battery box

Because the eight-cylinder engine takes up all the under-hood space, the battery is mounted in a separate box behind the driver's door.

Four-speed transmission

Even in the 1930s Alfas had four-speed transmissions while more ordinary cars had just three. There was no synchromesh, however, so the driver had to be skilled in matching engine revs to gear shifts.

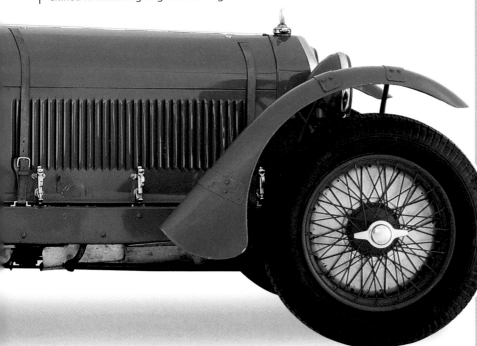

Specifications
1932 Alfa Romeo 8C 2300

ENGINE

Type: In-line eight cylinder
Construction: Alloy block and head with cast-iron liners
Valve gear: Two valves per cylinder operated by two gear-driven overhead cams
Bore and stroke: 2.56 in. x 3.33 in.
Displacement: 2,336 cc
Compression ratio: 5.75:1
Induction system: Single Memini updraft carburetor with Roots-type supercharger
Maximum power: 142 bhp at 5,200 rpm
Maximum torque: Not quoted
Top speed: 106 mph
0–60 mph: 9.4 sec.

TRANSMISSION

Four-speed manual

BODY/CHASSIS

Ladder frame chassis is three lengths and choice of coach-built bodywork

SPECIAL FEATURES

Much of the Alfa's power comes from the Roots-type supercharger which, like the overhead cams, is driven by the crankshaft.

Alfa's finned-alloy brakes fill the wheel rim and were very effective for their day.

RUNNING GEAR

Steering: Worm-and-wheel
Front suspension: Solid beam axle with semi-elliptic leaf springs and single friction shocks
Rear suspension: Live axle with semi-elliptic leaf springs and two friction shocks per side
Brakes: Drums, 15.5 in. dia. (front and rear), rod operated
Wheels: Wire spoke, 19-in. dia.
Tires: 5.5 in. x 19 in.

DIMENSIONS*

Length: 156 in. **Width:** 65 in.
Wheelbase: 107.9 in. **Height:** 44.2 in.
Track: 54 in. (front and rear)
Weight: 2,464 lbs.
*Vary according to body fitted, Figures for short chassis model

Alfa **ROMEO 8C 2900**

Alfa Romeo's 8C 2900 was the supercar of the 1930s. By using a leftover racing engine carrying twin superchargers, an all independently sprung chassis and clothing the whole lot in a variety of beautiful bodies, Alfa created one of the most desirable cars of all time.

"...the superchargers scream."

"The 8C 2900 was so good that the winning Alfa averaged over 86.8 mph over the 1,000-mile Mille Miglia race. As long as the swing-axle rear suspension is correctly set up the handling is excellent, thanks to the car's equal weight distribution and independent suspension which also gives a superb ride for a pre-war car. The Alfa engine gives loads of torque. Hit the throttle and hear the superchargers scream and all eight cylinders sing, amplified to a wonderful noise in the cockpit as you look over the long hood."

The vintage interior of 8C 2900 is very spartan. There is little to give away that it was one of the hottest supercars of the 1930s.

935 The first 8C 900 two-seater sports racer ppears. It runs a detuned P3 GP ght-cylinder engine.

936 Five more 8C 900s are built using the owerful 220-bhp engines.

agato bodywork clearly ows the design trends of the eriod.

937 The 8C 2900B is troduced. It is larger and eavier than the A models. They e available with a Corto (short) Lungo (long) chassis.

e supercharged engine gave utstanding performance.

938 A special treamlined 8C 2900 most wins the 24 Hours of Le ans.

939 The last 8C 900 is built just before 'orld War II. Total production 8C 2900Bs is 30.

947 An 8C 2900 Lungo upe, running without perchargers, wins the 1947 ille Miglia.

UNDER THE SKIN

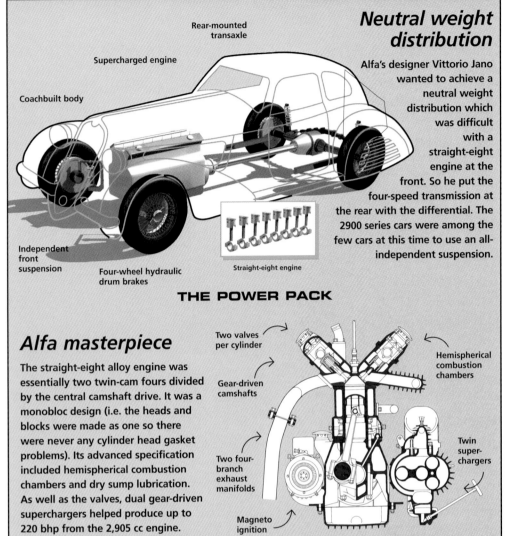

Rear-mounted transaxle

Supercharged engine

Coachbuilt body

Independent front suspension

Four-wheel hydraulic drum brakes

Straight-eight engine

Neutral weight distribution

Alfa's designer Vittorio Jano wanted to achieve a neutral weight distribution which was difficult with a straight-eight engine at the front. So he put the four-speed transmission at the rear with the differential. The 2900 series cars were among the few cars at this time to use an all-independent suspension.

THE POWER PACK

Alfa masterpiece

The straight-eight alloy engine was essentially two twin-cam fours divided by the central camshaft drive. It was a monobloc design (i.e. the heads and blocks were made as one so there were never any cylinder head gasket problems). Its advanced specification included hemispherical combustion chambers and dry sump lubrication. As well as the valves, dual gear-driven superchargers helped produce up to 220 bhp from the 2,905 cc engine.

Two valves per cylinder

Gear-driven camshafts

Two four-branch exhaust manifolds

Magneto ignition

Hemispherical combustion chambers

Twin superchargers

Coachbuilt

All 8C 2900 bodies were made by specialist coachbuilders rather than Alfa Romeo itself. Many were built by the likes of Pininfarina or Touring of Milan who made some of the most elegant and aerodynamic coupes in the world.

Some of the most beautiful 8C bodies were built by Touring of Milan.

Alfa ROMEO 8C 2900

Alfa 8C 2900s were produced in various styles. This one is a short chassis (Corto) with a convertible body built by Alfa Romeo rather than a famous outside specialist such as Touring of Milan.

Twin superchargers

Just as some modern supercars have twin turbos, the Alfa has two mechanically driven superchargers, each serving half the engine.

Coachbuilt body

Separate chassis, available in two different lengths, could carry a variety of body styles built by outside specialist coachbuilders.

Straight-eight engine

This is one of the greatest of pre-war engines, designed by Vittorio Jano and a development of his 2.3-liter straight-eight from the early 1930s. It's essentially a racing car engine detuned for the road.

Reverse gear lock-out

To avoid accidentally engaging reverse gear while driving, there is a lock-out mechanism. This feature was next used by Ferrari and can be found on most modern cars.

Swing-axle rear suspension

The Alfa has independent rear suspension but it is an unsophisticated system compared to those of today. With swing axles and a transverse spring it still has outstanding road holding for its day.

Rear-mounted transmission

To give a more neutral weight distribution both the transmission and differential were mounted at the rear in one unit. With the Alfa's straight-eight engine taking up all the room under the hood there was no room for the transmission at the front.

Hydraulic brakes

Many cars in the 1930s used mechanically operated brakes but the Alfa has large and efficient hydraulic drum brakes.

Hydraulic and friction shocks

Before the war hydraulic shocks were not as efficient as they are now and were sometimes supplemented with old-fashioned friction shocks.

Specifications
1938 Alfa Romeo 8C 2900B

ENGINE

Type: Straight-eight twin-cam
Construction: Alloy monobloc
Valve gear: Two valves per cylinder operated by twin overhead camshafts
Bore and stroke: 2.68 in. x 3.94 in.
Displacement: 2,905 cc
Compression ratio: 5.75:1
Induction system: Twin carburetors with twin Roots-type superchargers
Maximum power: 180 bhp at 5,200 rpm
Top speed: 115 mph
0–60 mph: 9.6 sec

TRANSMISSION

Four-speed manual, rear mounted

BODY/CHASSIS

Various styles on steel box section ladder frame with cross members

SPECIAL FEATURES

The gear drive to the camshafts is mounted in the center of the engine. This avoided having really long cams which would flex.

These vents are essential to reduce the engine bay temperature, especially in hot weather.

RUNNING GEAR

Steering: Worm-and-sector
Front suspension: Twin trailing arms per side with transverse arms operating coil spring/damper units
Rear suspension: Swing axles with trailing arms, semi-elliptic springs, hydraulic and friction shocks
Brakes: Drums all round
Wheels: Wire spoke 19-in. dia.
Tires: Crossply 5.50 in. x 19 in.

DIMENSIONS

Length: 174.4 in.   **Width:** 65.7 in.
Wheelbase: 110 in.   **Height:** 53.3 in.
Track: 53 in. (front and rear)
Weight: 2,519 lbs.

Amilcar **C6**

Designed to compete in small-capacity racing in the 1920s, the Amilcar's twin-cam, supercharged straight-six was a scaled-down GP version at only 1,094 cc, yet it produced enough power to reach over 100 mph.

"...shove in the back."

"Slide behind the wheel of the Amilcar and you know you're in a thoroughbred race car. The large wood-rimmed steering wheel lies in your lap and the many white-faced gauges sit in a beautiful, machine-turned alloy dashboard. The supercharged six howls like a demon, and the transmission whine is deafening. Performance is fantastic for a car with such a small engine—while the steering and handling are precise."

The machine-turned instrument panel harnesses a plethora of gauges.

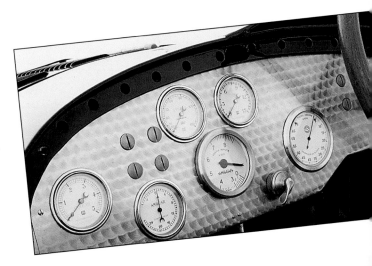

921 Designed by dmond Moyet and ndré Morel, the new Amilcar is tiny tax-beating cyclecar. The milcar venture is backed by sinessman Emil Akar, whose me was the inspiration for milcar. Morel sets a new class eed record of almost 60 mph r the flying kilometer.

e Amilcar was a highly ccessful competition car.

925 Having caught e racing bug, Morel signs a supercharged sixlinder twin-cam racing engine. tially known as the CO, the milcar racer is launched. It is tended as a production model.

fter the C6, Amilcar concenated its efforts on more vilized touring cars.

928 Production of e C6 Amilcar comes to an d. About 40 cars have reached ivate consumers.

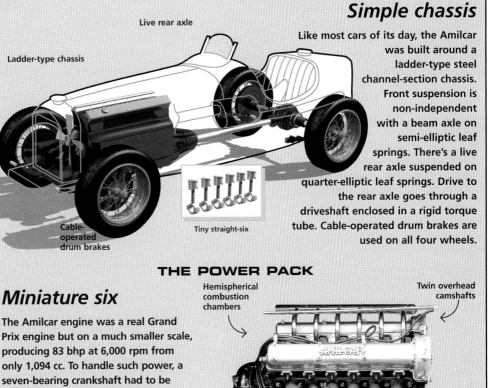

Live rear axle

Ladder-type chassis

Cable-operated drum brakes

Tiny straight-six

Simple chassis

Like most cars of its day, the Amilcar was built around a ladder-type steel channel-section chassis. Front suspension is non-independent with a beam axle on semi-elliptic leaf springs. There's a live rear axle suspended on quarter-elliptic leaf springs. Drive to the rear axle goes through a driveshaft enclosed in a rigid torque tube. Cable-operated drum brakes are used on all four wheels.

THE POWER PACK

Miniature six

The Amilcar engine was a real Grand Prix engine but on a much smaller scale, producing 83 bhp at 6,000 rpm from only 1,094 cc. To handle such power, a seven-bearing crankshaft had to be fitted. The cast-iron crankcase is a robust casting. A dry-sump lubrication system is used. Twin overhead camshafts actuate two valves per cylinder in hemispherical combustion chambers. The engine is supercharged with a twin-rotor, Roots-type blower that makes 12 psi. of boost.

Hemispherical combustion chambers

Twin overhead camshafts

Cast-iron block and head

Seven-bearing crankshaft

French fancy

With so few built, the Amilcar C6 is a real collector's car. Its purposeful styling and gem of an engine make it highly desirable both to own and to drive, whether on the road or dicing with other vintage racers on the track. The Amilcar is a Grand Prix car in miniature. Survivors have either been modified for racing or have been made a little more civilized for road use.

It is unlikely that any two surviving Amilcars are the same.

Amilcar **C6**

Six-cylinder Amilcars are among the rarest of pre-war classics. A mere 40 or so Amilcar C6s were assembled by the small, Paris-based manufacturer.

Beam front axle

Independent front suspension had no place in sports or racing cars in the 1920s. The customary system, as on the C6, was a beam axle joining both wheels. In the Amilcar's case the axle is underslung, with the ends cranked to keep the ride height as low as possible.

Twin-cam engine

The Amilcar C6 is powered by a tiny, 1,094-cc engine but despite the unit's size it has six cylinders. It was an advanced design with twin-overhead camshafts and hemispherical combustion chambers.

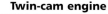

Twin-rotor supercharger

The six-cylinder engine's power is achieved with the use of a twin-rotor, Roots-type supercharger mounted at the front of the engine bay. Maximum boost is 12 psi, and the compression ratio low at 6.6:1.

Drum brakes

Large drum brakes were fitted to all four wheels. Although hydraulic brakes had been developed by this time, the Amilcar's drums were cable operated.

Front-mounted oil tank

In order to keep the overall height of the engine low, it is dry sumped and the oil is kept in a separate tank mounted between the front leaf springs.

...arter-elliptic leaf springs

...e all cars of its era, the C6 features a live rear axle, but ...tead of using the more usual semi-elliptic leaf springs it ...ocated and sprung by quarter-elliptic leaf springs, the ...ds of which are mounted outboard of the body.

Specifications
1928 Amilcar C6

ENGINE

Type: In-line six-cylinder

Construction: Cast-iron block and head

Valve gear: Two valves per cylinder operated by twin overhead camshafts

Bore and stroke: 2.20 in. x 2.91 in.

Displacement: 1,094 cc

Compression ratio: 6.6:1

Induction system: Single Solex carburetor with twin-rotor Roots-type supercharger

Maximum power: 83 bhp at 6,000 rpm

Maximum torque: Not quoted

Top speed: 105 mph

0–60 mph: 11.9 sec.

TRANSMISSION

Four-speed manual

BODY/CHASSIS

Steel ladder-type chassis with an aluminum two-seater open racing-type body

SPECIAL FEATURES

The Amilcar supercharger is driven off the end of the crankshaft.

The seven-bearing crankshaft is a superb piece of machining.

RUNNING GEAR

Steering: Worm-and-sector

Front suspension: Underslung beam axle with semi-elliptic leaf springs and Hartford friction shock absorbers

Rear suspension: Live axle with quarter-elliptic leaf springs and Hartford friction shock absorbers

Brakes: Drums (front and rear)

Wheels: Knock-off wire, 27-in. dia.

Tires: Dunlop, 4.40 x 27 in.

DIMENSIONS

Length: 133.9 in. **Width:** 50.4 in.

Height: 37.0 in. **Wheelbase:** 74.0 in.

Track: 44.3 in. (front and rear)

Weight: 1,567 lbs.

Aston Martin **C-TYPE**

Its streamlined body promised performance, and thanks to its advanced 110-bhp, 2-liter, overhead-cam engine, the C-Type did not disappoint. It was capable of nearly 100 mph.

"...high-speed stability."

"Stiff vintage-style springing makes the C-Type a hard-riding car, but to compensate for this harshness it offers superb handling. High-speed stability is also a strong point, the Aston taking full advantage of its aerodynamic lines. The steering is positive and direct. If the tail begins to break away it is easy to bring it back in line. The non-synchromesh transmission takes a bit of getting used to, but once mastered, becomes one of the car's strongest assets."

Fairly tight but functional, the C-Type's cockpit is nonetheless inviting.

Milestones

1938 Aston Martin exhibits a dramatically different style of bodywork at the Earls Court Show in London—the C-Type prototype. Under the new body is essentially the old 2-liter Speed Model first seen in 1936.

One of the most desirable of all 1930s Astons is the Ulster.

1939 Convinced that the prototype C-Type body is still not very unique, Aston Martin radically changes the design, moving the headlamps inboard behind a new wire mesh grill and gives the whole car a modern streamlined look. Seven cars are built to this pattern.

The 15/98 Short used a detuned 2-liter engine.

1940 The last of the C-Types find buyers, but by this time, Britain is already at war with Germany, and all civilian car production ceases.

UNDER THE SKIN

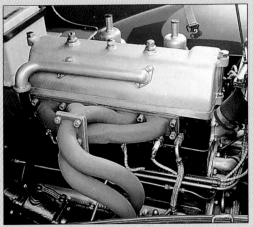

Beam axles front and rear

Dual-circuit hydraulic drum brakes

Separate ladder-type chassis frame

Proven inline four

High-tech brakes

The 2-liter Speed Model, on which the C-Type was based, wasn't completely up to date by 1938. The chassis was a conventional ladder frame. The chassis rails go under the live back axle, which used semi-elliptic leaf springs. Front suspension was equally old-fashioned, with a beam axle, again on leaf springs. The one really modern feature was the superb dual-circuit hydraulic braking system.

THE POWER PACK

Veteran engine

Although there was little new about the engine, this 2-liter four-cylinder is a wonderful design, with a gear- and chain-driven overhead camshaft working two valves per cylinder. The layout is crossflow but very unusual, with the valves inline across the head, at an angle to form a wedge-shaped (and very efficient) combustion chamber. Unlike most engines, the intake valve is positioned below the exhaust valve. A single tubular exhaust manifold helps expel the spent exhaust gases more efficiently than less restrictive designs, and helps the engine crank out its maximum of 110 bhp.

Old or bold?

Few cars polarized opinion as much as the C-Type. Some saw it as a sham—an old car with a new and controversial-looking body. Others saw it as a bold statement of the way in which car design should go. Although not widely appreciated when new, the C-Type certainly is today.

The last of the C-Types were sold in 1940.

25

Aston Martin **C-TYPE**

The bold styling with its exaggerated long rear fenders and tail contrasted with a large, blunt nose to produce a shape that many thought looked very unbalanced. Its visual impact was undeniable when it appeared, however.

Four-cylinder engine

Designed to be revved hard and for long periods, the 2-liter, overhead-cam four was made as strong as possible despite having just three main bearings. The crankshaft was nitrided to give the hardest, most wear-resistant finish, and there was a mechanical drive to the generator. A four-branch exhaust manifold allowed the engine to breathe easier.

Steel superstructure

On top of the traditional chassis frame, Aston Martin erected small square-section steel tube framework. This served the same purpose as the old-fashioned wooden ash frame used by English coachbuilders, but was stronger and helped overall stiffness.

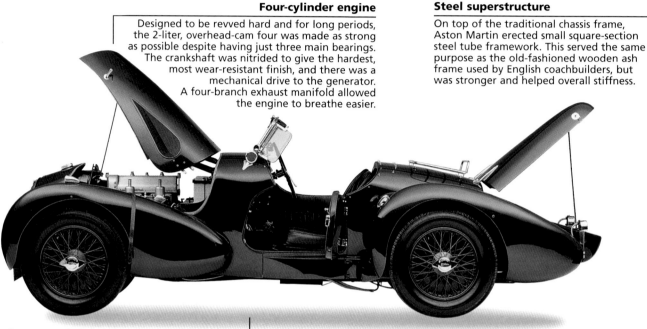

Dry-sump lubrication

To prevent oil starvation during racing the engine had dry-sump lubrication. All the oil is held in a separate tank and pumped to and from the engine. The oil tank is mounted at the front of the car and doubles as an oil cooler.

Wind deflectors

One interesting feature is the dual-purpose windshield. When the main windshield is raised, the smaller windows also double as side deflectors.

Streamlined front

Part of the reason for the very advanced-looking alloy bodywork over the tubular-steel frame was to make what was basically an old car look modern. Another reason was aircraft-style aerodynamics.

Specifications

1939 Aston Martin C-Type

ENGINE
Type: Inline four-cylinder
Construction: Cast-iron block and head
Valve gear: Two valves per cylinder operated by a single chain-driven overhead camshaft
Bore and stroke: 3.07 in. x 4.02 in.
Displacement: 1,950 cc
Compression ratio: 8.25:1
Induction system: Two SU carburetors
Maximum power: 110 bhp at 5,500 rpm
Maximum torque: Not quoted
Top speed: 97 mph
0–60 mph: 15.4 sec.

TRANSMISSION
Four-speed manual

BODY/CHASSIS
Separate underslung ladder-type frame with steel superstructure and alloy two-seater convertible body

SPECIAL FEATURES

Dual carburetors help add a few extra bhp on the track.

The four-speed transmission did not feature synchromesh, requiring the driver to double declutch.

RUNNING GEAR
Steering: Cam-and-peg
Front suspension: Beam axle with semi-elliptic leaf springs and friction shock absorbers
Rear suspension: Live axle with semi-elliptic leaf springs and friction shock absorbers
Brakes: Ribbed drums, 14-in. dia.
Wheels: Knock-on/off center-fixing wire spoke, 18-in. dia.
Tires: 5.25 x 18

DIMENSIONS
Length: 168.0 in.   **Width:** 64.0 in.
Height: 55.0 in.   **Wheelbase:** 102.0 in.
Track: 54.5 in. (front and rear)
Weight: 2,567 lbs.

Auburn SPEEDSTER

Auburn's 851 Speedster was the sleekest car on American roads in the 1930s. It followed the lead of the big Mercedes SSK of the 1920s with its supercharged engine, and its eight cylinders were enough to give a guaranteed top speed of more than 100 mph.

"The faster the better."

"That was the opinion of road testers in 1935. In America that year there was nothing to touch the Auburn Speedster for the price. The supercharged 280-cubic inch eight-cylinder engine gives lots of smooth power, and thanks to the two-speed axle and three-speed transmission, the driver has six gears to play with. The hydraulic brakes are man enough to haul the heavy car down, and the handling is impressive for its day. Because of its low-geared steering and excessive body roll, the car shows its age around tight corners."

The Auburn Speedster offered a high level of comfort as well as serious art-deco fittings.

Milestones

1928 First Auburn 'boat tail' Speedster is introduced. It has a similar tiny swept-back windshield, but an upright grill and open fenders. Most powerful is the eight-cylinder, 125-bhp 8-125, produced in 1930.

This 1929 Model 115 evolved into the 120 and the 125.

1932 By adding a 160-bhp Lycoming V12 to the speedster chassis, Auburn creates the similarly styled 12-160 Speedster. Top speed is 117 mph but it is not a success and is dropped for 1934.

1935 The Speedster 851 is introduced. Restyled by new designer, Gordon Buehrig, it uses a 150-bhp supercharged version of the Lycoming straight-eight engine.

Auburn's dynamic president, Errett Lobban Cord, arrived at Auburn in 1924.

1936 Name changes to 852 from 851. Sales are low and production ends. The total number of 851/852 speedsters built is just over 500.

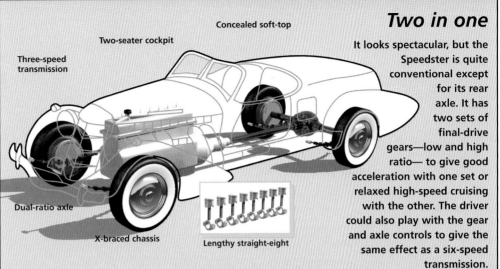

Concealed soft-top
Two-seater cockpit
Three-speed transmission
Dual-ratio axle
X-braced chassis
Lengthy straight-eight

Two in one

It looks spectacular, but the Speedster is quite conventional except for its rear axle. It has two sets of final-drive gears—low and high ratio— to give good acceleration with one set or relaxed high-speed cruising with the other. The driver could also play with the gear and axle controls to give the same effect as a six-speed transmission.

THE POWER PACK

Eight supercharged cylinders

Built by Lycoming, better known for its aircraft engines, the Speedster's engine was not advanced—a simple side-valve design, it was a vintage layout for such a sporty engine. But with a mechanically driven supercharger running at four pounds of boost, the straight-eight engine gives a good deal of low-end torque. Although the centrifugal supercharger runs at six times crankshaft speed, the limited amount of boost means the engine is hardly over-stressed.

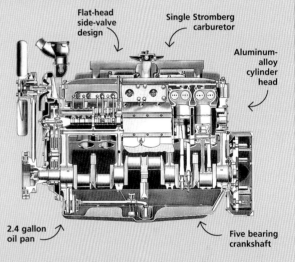

Flat-head side-valve design
Single Stromberg carburetor
Aluminum-alloy cylinder head
2.4 gallon oil pan
Five bearing crankshaft

Auburn record

In 1935, the classy Auburn Speedster became the first American production car to exceed 100 mph for more than 12 hours, averaging 102.9 mph. It was driven by racing driver Ab Jenkins. He also set a new record in the flying mile with a top speed of 104.17 mph.

Using a centrifugal supercharger, the Speedster really lives up to its name.

Auburn SPEEDSTER

Auburn's famous designer Gordon Buehrig wanted the Speedster to appear to be the fastest car on the road. He succeeded, using features like the low V windshield, sloping grill and flowing wing-line to give a streamlined look to the car.

Teardrop headlights

The Auburn's styling is supposed to suggest speed. The streamlined lights, with bulging convex lenses, help achieve this impression.

Supercharged engine

The Auburn's mechanically driven supercharger runs at six times engine-speed and helps the Lycoming engine generate 150 bhp—35 bhp more than without the supercharger.

Top cover

The Auburn's top folds away neatly under this rigid cover to maintain the car's sleek lines.

Flexible exhaust headers

Each of the four flexible exhaust headers serve two cylinders. The conventional rigid pipes are hidden under the flexible tubes.

Dual-ratio rear axle

The driver could switch from a low- to a high- axle ratio, and with a three-speed transmission that gave six gears overall. In high-ratio top gear, the Speedster's engine rotated at only 2,250 rpm at 60 mph.

Winged mascots

Each of the side 'flying lady' mascots was made by slicing the radiator mascot in two.

Luggage hatch

A carriage key opens this hatch. The compartment is just large enough to take a set of golf clubs, a feature much appreciated by the typical playboy Speedster owner.

Hydraulic lever-arm shocks

Before telescopic shocks were introduced, cars like the Auburn used hydraulic lever arms to replace the previous friction shocks.

Drum brakes

All the cars in the 1930s had drum brakes, but the Auburn's hydraulically-operated drums were more modern than most.

Boat-tail design

From above, the description is obvious. The style was popular in the 1920s and '30s and here it is mirrored in in its rearend styling.

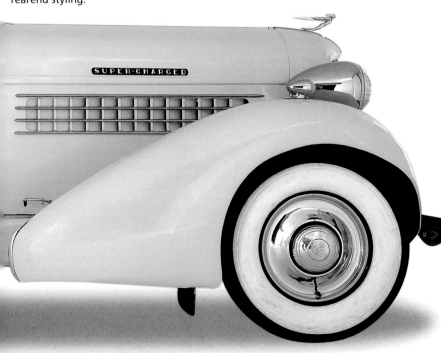

Specifications
1935 Auburn Speedster 851

ENGINE

Type: In-line eight
Construction: Cast-iron block and light alloy cylinder head
Valve gear: Side-valve with two valves per cylinder and single block-mounted camshaft
Bore and stroke: 3.06 in. x 4.75 in.
Displacement: 280 c.i.
Compression ratio: 6.5:1
Induction system: Single downdraft Stromberg carburetor with Schwitzer-Cummins supercharger
Maximum power: 150 bhp at 4,000 rpm
Top speed: 108 mph
0–50 mph: 10.0 sec.

TRANSMISSION

Three-speed manual with dual-ratio rear axle

BODY/CHASSIS

Steel two-door, two-seat speedster body with steel box-section ladder-type chassis rails

SPECIAL FEATURES

Each Speedster has a signed plaque guaranteeing it has been tested to more than 100 mph.

Mechanically-driven supercharger is used to boost power.

RUNNING GEAR

Steering: Worm-and-peg
Front suspension: Solid axle with semi-elliptic leaf springs and Delco hydraulic shock absorbers
Rear suspension: Live axle with semi-elliptic leaf springs and Delco hydraulic shock absorbers
  Brakes: Four-wheel Lockheed drums, hydraulically operated with Bendix vacuum booster
  Wheels: Pressed steel or wire spoke, 6.5 in. x 15 in.
Tires: Crossply 6.5 in. x 16 in.

DIMENSIONS

Length: 194.4 in. **Width:** 71.5 in.
Height: 56.5 in. **Wheelbase:** 127 in.
Track: 59 in. (front), 62 in. (rear)
Weight: 3,753 lbs.

Austin **SEVEN**

With the Seven, Sir Herbert Austin was doing exactly what Henry Ford had done with the Model T; he introduced a simple, tough and reliable car that was affordable.

"...plenty of charm."

"The steering is direct and light, so any movement the car makes can instantly be corrected. Although the engine is small, it feels tough and eager when tuned. The transmission fitted to the racier Ulster and homebuilt special models is much quicker and easier to use. The ride is firm, and despite the low speeds, you need your wits about you because the brake pedal must be pressed before you actually need to stop."

There is a healthy measure of character to the sparse interior of the Seven.

Milestones

1922 The Austin Seven becomes the smallest four-cylinder-engined car available on the British market.

Early Sevens—here a 1927 Chummy—were rudimentary.

1923 Engine size is increased to 747-cc and the bigger powerplant gets an electric starter and a cooling fan.

1929 After the range has been steadily expanded through the Sports Tourer and the Sedan, the lowered and far more sporty Ulster model appears. Its performance can be hugely increased with an optional Cozette supercharger.

Austin Sevens were still very popular in 1935.

1939 Even the Austin Seven cannot stay in production forever and the last one is built in January. By this time, more than 290,000 have been produced.

UNDER THE SKIN

Transverse leaf-sprung front suspension

Drum brakes front and rear

Separate steel-arm-frame chassis

Inline four

THE POWER PACK

Simple Seven

The idea was to make the Seven as simple as possible, so the two main chassis rails meet at the front under the engine and at the middle of the beam front axle. The front suspension is by a transverse leaf spring, and the live rear axle has quarter-elliptic leaf springs. Only a couple of crossmembers are needed to brace the structure. The four-wheel brakes are tiny drums and are cable operated.

Interesting design

It was a surprise to see a proper four-cylinder engine in a car so small, and the result is technically interesting. There is a cast-iron block with an alloy crankcase to keep weight down. The short crankshaft runs on just two main bearings, but these are roller bearings rather than the white metal-type, and rely on oil splash from the sump to keep them lubricated. The block holds eight inline side valves operating upward onto the iron head and there is a single block-mounted camshaft. Power figures are not earth-shattering, but 12 bhp was respectable for the day.

Racers

The most sought after Sevens are the Ulsters, so called after an incredible performance in the 1929 Ulster TT race. The tuned engine produces about 24 bhp, but the supercharged version pumps out 33 bhp, enough for a top speed of 75 mph.

Light and simple, the Seven became a favorite for special builders everywhere.

Austin SEVEN

This Austin Seven Special looks a world apart from the day-to-day sedans and tourers. Its minimal, doorless, two-seater sports racing bodywork is designed to be as light as possible to make the most of the performance.

Sidevalve engine

When the 747-cc inline sidevalve four was reengineered in 1936, it was given a third main bearing. At the same time, the head was redesigned to give more efficient combustion and power.

Live rear axle

The live rear axle has quarter-elliptic leaf springs and is mounted on the ends of the main chassis rails.

Gravity-feed tank

Early Austin Seven engines had their fuel fed to them by a gas tank, located under the scuttle and behind the engine. From there, gravity alone shifted the fuel to the single Zenith updraft carburetor. The tank was moved to the rear late in the car's life.

Three-speed transmission

Initially, only a three-speed transmission was offered. More than 10 years later, the car was given a four-speed that was soon improved with synchromesh.

Worm-and-sector steering

The Seven requires little effort to steer through the worm-and-sector system, as the car is so light and runs on very narrow, high-pressure tires.

Wire wheels

The Seven could get by with such spindly wire wheels because the tire size is narrow, the car is light, and the performance, both in acceleration and braking, is so low. Wheel size varied over time, with some cars having 15-inch rims and others having 19-inch rims.

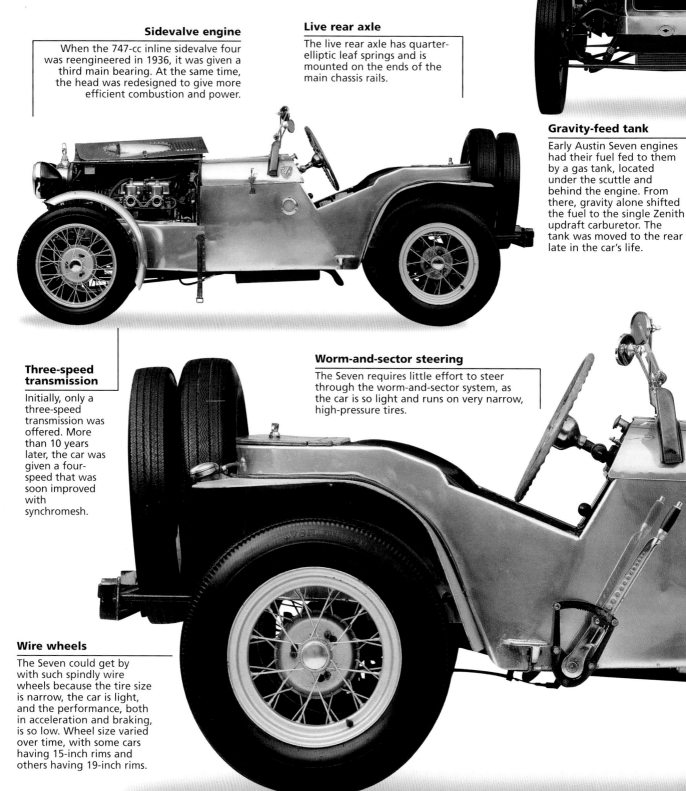

Beam front axle

To keep the front suspension cheap and simple, it consists of a solid beam, which is suspended by a transverse semi-elliptic leaf spring above it. Location is provided by two radius arms running back from the hubs to a point behind the engine.

Specifications

1930 Austin Seven

ENGINE
Type: Inline four-cylinder
Construction: Cast-iron block and head
Valve gear: Two inline sidevalves per cylinder operated by a single block-mounted camshaft
Bore and stroke: 2.24 in. x 3.04 in.
Displacement: 747 cc
Compression ratio: 4.8:1
Induction system: Single Zenith updraft carburetor
Maximum power: 12 bhp at 2,600 rpm
Maximum torque: Not quoted
Top speed: 66 mph
0–60 mph: Not quoted

TRANSMISSION
Three-speed manual

BODY/CHASSIS
Separate steel chassis with wood, fabric and steel bodywork

SPECIAL FEATURES

This Special features twin carburetors in place of the single Zenith.

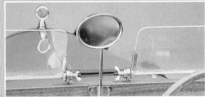

Twin aero screens are the only protection for driver and passenger.

RUNNING GEAR
Steering: Worm-and-sector
Front suspension: Beam axle with transverse semi-elliptic leaf spring, radius arms and friction shock absorbers
Rear suspension: Live axle with torque tube, quarter-elliptic leaf springs, radius arms and friction shock absorbers
Brakes: Drums (front and rear)
Wheels: Wire spoke
Tires: Beaded edge

DIMENSIONS
Length: 106.0 in.   **Width:** 46.0 in.
Height: 55.2 in.   **Wheelbase:** 75.0 in.
Track: 40.0 in. (front and rear)
Weight: 952 lbs.

Bentley **4½ LITRE**

Built to be unbreakable, the 4½ Litre thundered around for 24 hours to win Le Mans in 1928 and featured advanced engine technology behind that massive radiator grill.

"...hustled around corners."

"Although the 4½ Litre is heavy it is also well-balanced and the steering quick and precise. Despite the crude-sounding specification the Bentley can be hustled around corners quickly and will easily cruise at 90 mph. The biggest trick to driving it is mastering the non-synchro transmission. Once mastered, however, it's easy to exploit the real power of the Bentley. The weight of the heavy supercharger right at the front turns the 'Blower' Bentley into a determined understeer."

Gauges, gauges everywhere. The Bentley 4½ Litre has gauges for everything set into its beautiful alloy dashboard.

Milestones

1927 Prototype 4½ litre car appears at the Le Mans 24 Hours but goes out in the infamous White House crash.

1928 4½ Litre wins Le Mans, averaging 69 mph, despite running at the end with no water left in the engine.

W. O. Bentley disapproved of supercharging.

1929 4½ Litre of Dunfee/Kidson finishes second at Le Mans behind the winning 6½ Litre Bentley.

1930 First of the supercharged 'Blower' Bentleys is built, a venture by Bentley driver Tim Birkin without W. O. Bentley's support. Engine is designed and the supercharger installation is designed by Amherst Villiers.

1932 Tim Birkin's 'Blower' Bentley breaks the outer circuit lap record at Brooklands with a lap at 135 mph.

Tim Birkin at the wheel of a supercharged 'Blower' Bentley.

UNDER THE SKIN

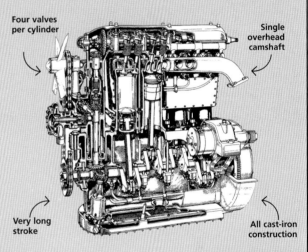

Transmission separate from engine

Sturdy separate chassis

Enormous straight-four

Four-wheel drum brakes

Fastest lorry

All of W. O. Bentley's cars were massively engineered and the 4½ Litre has an extremely strong ladder frame chassis to support the heavy engine, which is actually separated from the transmission. It is closer to the middle of the car, virtually under the dashboard. The Bentley followed common practice by using huge drum brakes, a solid front axle and semi-elliptic leaf springs for the suspension.

THE POWER PACK

Sixteen valve

Although the big four-cylinder is all cast-iron, tall and narrow with a very-long stroke to give a large (although undisclosed) amount of torque, one feature of the 4½ Litre engine still seems modern. It has four valves per cylinder, angled at 30 degrees, and all operated by a single overhead camshaft via a system of rocker arms. The camshaft is driven off the crankshaft via a vertical shaft and bevel gears so there is no chain to break. The 4½ Litre produces 110 bhp when naturally aspirated.

Four valves per cylinder

Single overhead camshaft

Very long stroke

All cast-iron construction

'Blowers'

Although W. O. Bentley vehemently disapproved of supercharging, it's the 54 'Blower' Bentleys which are most famous and desirable, despite their poor competition record. Many Bentley sedans have been converted into 'Blower' replicas.

Supercharged 'Blower' Bentleys are the most desirable of the 4½ Litre cars.

Bentley 4½ LITRE

When W. O. Bentley wanted more power from his cars he made the engines bigger, moving up to 6½ and then 8.0 liters. Ironically the supercharged car he disapproved of so much has become the most famous.

Solid beam front axle

All of W. O. Bentley's cars had a solid beam axle located and sprung by two semi-elliptic leaf springs, along with friction shock absorbers.

Center lock wheels

Tire changes could be made quickly in the pits because the Rudge Whitworth wheels have a single knock-off center fixing, undone with a soft-faced hammer.

Worm-and-wheel steering

The Bentley has a worm-and-wheel. The driver's side wheel is linked to the steering mechanism and a bar from that wheel runs under the chassis to the other front wheel.

Fold-down windshield

Although the Bentley had the aerodynamics of a barn door, the windshield can be folded flat and the small aero-window erected to slightly improve the car's aerodynamics.

Massive brakes

It's heavy and fast, requiring 17-inch brakes that are ribbed for cooling. Although Duesenberg had pioneered hydraulic brakes, the Bentley's are cable operated.

Stone guards

The world's race tracks were neither as smooth nor stone-free as today's. To prevent damage Bentley used stone guards to protect the exposed carburetors next to the supercharger and the fuel tank at the rear.

External handbrake

There was no room inside the cockpit for the externally-mounted handbrake lever. Even the gearshifter isn't in the middle of the cockpit, but off to the driver's side.

No driver's door

With the side cutaway to allow the driver to move his elbows there was no need for a door.

Live rear axle

Like all its rivals of the era, the Bentley uses a simple live axle, located and sprung on two semi-elliptic leaf springs.

Specifications
1930 Bentley 4½ Litre supercharged

ENGINE

Type: In-line four cylinder
Construction: Cast-iron block and head
Valve gear: Four valves per cylinder operated by single gear-and shaft-driven overhead camshafts
Bore and stroke: 3.93 in. x 5.51 in.
Displacement: 4,398 cc
Compression ratio: 5.0:1
Induction system: Two SU carburetors with Amherst Villiers Roots-type supercharger
Maximum power: 175 bhp at 3,500 rpm
Maximum power (racing): 240 bhp at 2,400 rpm
Maximum torque: not quoted
Top speed: 125 mph
0–60 mph: Not quoted

TRANSMISSION

Four-speed manual

BODY/CHASSIS

Steel ladder frame with cross bracing, and open steel and fabric body

SPECIAL FEATURES

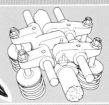

The Roots-type supercharger drives off the crankshaft. Two lobes are rotated, drawing air and fuel through the carburetors, compressing it and forcing it through the intake manifold and into the engine.

Bentley used four-valve technology as early as 1919, and continued it in the 4½ Litre's engine.

RUNNING GEAR

Steering: Worm-and-wheel
Front suspension: Solid beam axle with leaf springs and shocks
Rear suspension: Live axle with semi-elliptic leaf springs and shocks
Brakes: Four-wheel drums
Wheels: Rudge Whitworth 6 in. x 20in.
Tires: Dunlop crossply, 6 in. x 20 in.

DIMENSIONS

Length: 172.5 in. **Width:** 68.5 in.
Height: 63 in. **Wheelbase:** 130 in.
Track: 54.49 in. (front and rear)
Weight: 4,235 lbs.

Bentley 8-LITRE

It never won, or was even entered, in the 24 Hours of Le Mans race but the 8-Litre was arguably the best of all the genuine Bentleys before the Rolls-Royce takeover. It had the biggest engine, best chassis and most power and performance.

"...unimaginable power."

"Forget the four valves per cylinder because there's nothing modern about the massive 8-Litre. The gear shift is extremely awkward from first to second, and initially the steering is extraordinarily heavy. It's out of place on a narrow lane, but once the big Bentley is on an open road it comes alive. There is unimaginable power and torque. Its massive size gives a serene ride, and if pushed, the 8-Litre will storm through curves quickly with perfect stability."

Superb craftsmanship has long been a trademark of Bentleys, inside and out.

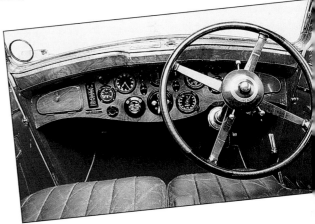

930 Bentley wins

Mans for the fifth time, but stead of going from strength strength, the company is in minal financial trouble due to or sales. Despite this, Bentley veils the great 8-Litre at ndon's Olympia Show.

record-breaking 8-Litre was e Forrest Lycett car.

931 With the ankrupt company taken

ver by Rolls-Royce, 8-Litre oduction is stopped. Rolls has need for the model, as it ready produces the Phantom. nly a mere 100 8-Litres have en made.

variety of coachbuilt bodies ere fitted to 8-Litre chassis.

959 Now nearly 0 years old, the heavily odified Forrest Lycett 8-Litre is ken to Belgium for yet nother record attempt. It vers the flying mile at 140.845 ph to show just how great a r the 8-Litre could be.

UNDER THE SKIN

Massive chassis

Massive steel-beam chassis

Solid front and rear axles

Servo assisted drum brakes

Huge inline eight

The 8-Litre Bentleys are massive. The huge side chassis rails and cross-members carry an equally massive live rear axle located and suspended on semi-elliptic leaf springs with friction shocks. The front axle was also solid, again located by semi-elliptic leaf springs and friction shocks. Huge finned alloy brake drums with Dewandre servo assistance were needed to stop one of the heaviest and fastest cars on the road at the time.

THE POWER PACK

Multivalve engine

W.O. Bentley was more interested in a powerful engine than in the rest of the car, and the straight-six 8-liter is a fine example. It was an evolution of the firm's famous 6$\frac{1}{2}$-liter block and drew heavily on Bentley's racing experience. The head and block were made in one iron casting to avoid any head gasket problems. There were still four valves per cylinder in hemispherical combustion chambers, operated by a single overhead camshaft and rockers. The camshaft is driven off of the crankshaft to avoid the noise of a chain. Fuel was fed in through twin SU carburetors.

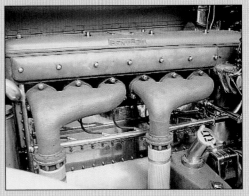

Speed records

The most famous of all 8-Litres is the Forrest Lycett car, which set a standing kilometer record. Because only 100 8-Litres were built, and since it was the last of the 'true' Bentleys, any example of this model commands substantial prices today.

A huge displacement made the 8-Litre one of the fastest cars of its time.

Bentley 8-LITRE

The enormous engine was developed by Bentley because its customers would insist on fitting their cars with the largest and heaviest bodies available. Such was the power of the 8-Litre that weight did not matter.

Twin spark ignition

In some very large combustion chambers, Bentley used a twin-spark ignition. The spark plugs were mounted horizontally below the valves on each side of the block. One set was fired by a magneto, the other set using a coil.

Straight-six engine

The biggest Bentley engine was basically the same as that used for the Speed Six 6.6-liter engine, but with the bore increased to give 8 liters. That still made it a very long-stroke (4.33-inch x 5.51-inch) design, and the engine was very tall and narrow.

Coachbuilt bodywork

Bentley was more interested in supplying the chassis than a complete car. An 8-Litre customer would have his car bodied by any one of a number of great outside coachbuilders like Mulliner or Vanden Plas.

Solid front axle

Bentley was not interested in experiments with independent front suspension and stayed with a solid axle with a semi-elliptic leaf spring system along with adjustable friction-type shocks.

Drum brakes

One advantage of having tall wheels (21 inches) is for the enormous brake drums. They need to be big to stop the car. They have finned alloy casings and are operated with a rod.

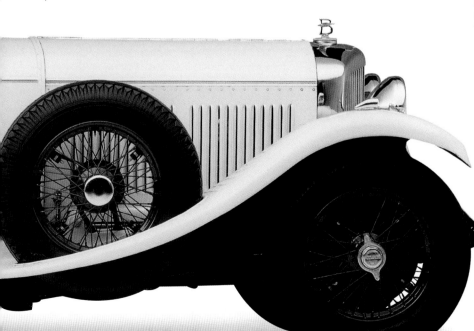

Specifications
1930 Bentley 8-Litre

ENGINE

Type: Inline six-cylinder
Construction: Integral cast-iron cylinder block and head with separate crankcase and sump
Valve gear: Four valves per cylinder operated by single overhead camshaft driven by three shafts and gears from the crankshaft
Bore and stroke: 4.33 in. x 5.51 in.
Displacement: 7,982 cc
Compression ratio: 5.3:1
Induction system: Two SU carburetors
Maximum power: 225 bhp at 3,500 rpm
Maximum torque: N/A
Top speed: 101 mph
0–60 mph: N/A

TRANSMISSION

Four-speed manual

BODY/CHASSIS

Separate steel channel-section chassis with two side members and tubular cross-members with choice of bodywork

SPECIAL FEATURES

Flip-out, semaphore-type turn signals are mounted on the sides of the trunk.

As on previous Bentleys, the parking brake and shifter are mounted on the right side.

RUNNING GEAR

Steering: Worm-and-wheel
Front suspension: Solid axle with semi-elliptic leaf springs and friction shocks
Rear suspension: Live axle with semi-elliptic leaf springs and friction shocks
Brakes: Finned drums (front and rear), servo-assisted
Wheels: Quick-release knock-on/off wire spoke, 21-in. dia.
Tires: Crossply 21-in. dia.

DIMENSIONS

Length: 200.5 in.   **Width:** 69.4 in.
Height: 71.5 in.   **Wheelbase:** 144.0 in.
Track: 55.9 in. (front and rear)
Weight: 5,390 lbs.

BMW 328

The BMW 328 was the best small sports car built before the war. When it first appeared in 1936 its combination of sensational looks, sharp handling, and spritely performance was unrivaled.

"...amazingly modern."

"It is a tight squeeze behind the large-diameter steering wheel, but the 328 feels more modern than a 1930s car. It is also a wonderfully precise car, with superb steering and near viceless handling. The brakes, too, are excellent, and there is plenty of grip: a well-driven 328 will keep pace with many modern cars along twisty roads. The 2.0-liter hemi-head engine has good power throughout the range, but the transmission is fragile."

The painted metal dashboard is typical of German design of the period.

1928 BMW moves into the car market with the acquisition of Dixi, which builds Austin Sevens under license.

The postwar AC Ace uses a Bristol version of the 328 engine.

1934 The company launches a car of its own design. The 315 is installed with 55-bhp, 1,490-cc straight-six engine and twin-tube chassis.

The earlier BMW 326 has the same engine block as the 328.

1936 The 328 is introduced. A new cylinder head increases the power of the six-cylinder engine to 80 bhp.

1940 A 328 wins the Mille Miglia road race. Production ceases as World War commences.

UNDER THE SKIN

Stiff and strong

Tubular-steel ladder-type chassis

Independent front suspension

Hydraulic drum brakes all around

Advanced six-cylinder

The 328 really scores over its contemporaries in the marriage of a stiff chassis, relatively soft suspension, accurate steering, and hydraulic drum brakes. The chassis is a tubular-steel ladder-type frame, which is lighter and more rigid than the more usual channel-section ladder-type chassis. It has independent front suspension with a single transverse leaf spring and a live rear axle. Hydraulic shocks and drum brakes are fitted all around.

THE POWER PACK

Hemi-head six

The 328 is powered by BMW's pre-war straight-six engine which has a special aluminum cylinder head with hemispherical combustion chambers. In order to operate the inclined valves using only a single camshaft, the engine uses ingenious short cross-over pushrods. Unusually for the period the camshaft is chain-driven, whereas most camshafts in the 1930s were gear-driven. With a 7.5:1 compression ratio and using three downdraft Solex carburetors, the 328 engine produces 80 bhp.

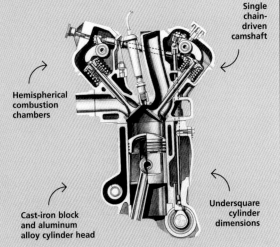

Single chain-driven camshaft

Hemispherical combustion chambers

Cast-iron block and aluminum alloy cylinder head

Undersquare cylinder dimensions

Streamliner

The most desirable 328s are the five cars built for the 1940 Mille Miglia. Three of these are lightweight aerodynamic roadsters. The other two are the winning Touring of Milan-built coupe and a peculiar-looking aerodynamic coupe.

BMW built several aerodynamic 328s especially for racing.

BMW 328

The 328 was light, nimble and, with 80 bhp, powerful enough to form the basis of a successful competition car. It was also an excellent sports car.

Triple carburetors

The 328 has a high bodyline because the straight-six engine is fed by three downdraft Solex carburetors mounted above it. The 328's unique valve gear leaves no room for side-mounted carburetors.

Tubular-steel chassis

Built before monocoque construction became commonplace, the 328 uses a simple tubular-steel chassis. The two main longitudinal chassis members are wide-based at the rear and angled inward toward the front.

Rack-and-pinion steering

The 328 has very direct handling, partly due to the car's high-geared steering. The use of rack-and-pinion steering was very advanced for the 1930s.

Hemi-head straight-six

The 2.0-liter straight-six engine has only one block-mounted camshaft, but it still has hemispherical combustion chambers with inclined valves.

Excellent brakes

The 328 has hydraulically-operated drums all around. These are very effective and helped by the car's light weight.

Specifications
1937 BMW 328

ENGINE

Type: In-line six

Construction: Cast-iron block and aluminum alloy head

Valve gear: Two valves per cylinder operated by a single camshaft via pushrods and rockers; inlet valves operated directly, exhaust valves by cross-over pushrods

Bore and stroke: 2.6 in. x 3.8 in.

Displacement: 1,971 cc

Compression ratio: 7.5:1

Induction system: Three downdraft Solex carburetors

Maximum power: 80 bhp at 4,500 rpm

Maximum torque: 93 lb-ft at 4,000 rpm

Top speed: 103 mph

0–60 mph: 9.5 sec.

TRANSMISSION

Four-speed manual

BODY/CHASSIS

Tubular-steel ladder-type chassis with two-seater open sports body

SPECIAL FEATURES

The spare wheel is mounted on the trunk to give more luggage space.

These leather retaining straps hold the hood closed.

RUNNING GEAR

Steering: Rack-and-pinion

Front suspension: Independent with lower wishbones, transverse semi-elliptic leaf spring and lever-arm shocks

Rear suspension: Live axle with semi-elliptic leaf springs and lever-arm shocks

Brakes: Drums, 11-in. dia. (front and rear)

Wheels: Knock-on pressed-steel discs

Tires: Crossply, 5.25 x 16 in.

DIMENSIONS

Length: 153.5 in.   **Width:** 61 in.

Height: 49 in.   **Wheelbase:** 93 in.

Track: 45.5 in. (front), 48 in. (rear)

Weight: 1,638 lbs.

Bugatti **TYPE 35**

It was one of the most successful racing cars of all time, with nearly 2,000 wins to its credit. The Type 35 could also be driven on the road, however, just like a normal sports car.

"...incredibly responsive."

"With such a tremendous amount of power going through such narrow tires, it is no surprise that the Type 35B takes some getting used to. The car's light steering is incredibly responsive and the handling is beautifully balanced; it's controlled by the throttle as much as the steering. Changing gears requires a quick, firm action and a delicate clutch foot. The brakes, though quite antiquated, work well too, if you push hard enough."

Despite its reputation as a sports car, the Type 35 has no creature comforts.

924 Ettore Bugatti nveils his new Type 35 cer in time for the French rand Prix. Tire trouble prevents win.

...ugatti also built huge luxury ...rs like the famous Royale.

925 Bugatti's five- ear domination of the Targa orio road race begins.

925 The lower- owered Type 35A ...pears. A 1.5-liter derivative of e 35, the Type 39 was unveiled 1926.

...is twin-cam Type 51 is at the ...31 Monaco Grand Prix.

926 Supercharging e 2.0-liter straight- ...ght produces the Type 35C. The ...27 35B has a supercharged 2.3- ...er engine with an output of ...0 bhp.

930 Type 35 production ...ds. The twin-cam Type 51 ...velopment takes over its ...and Prix role.

UNDER THE SKIN

Light and strong

The two main chassis rails are of varying depth according to the stress they receive at each point and are joined by crossmembers to form a very rigid structure. A live rear axle is sprung by reversed quarter-elliptic springs and located by radius arms for good location, while the front axle looks solid but is actually hollow to save weight. It is mounted on semi-, rather than quarter-, elliptic springs.

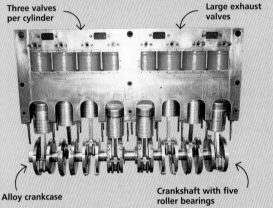

Live rear axle

All-leaf-sprung suspension

Ladder-type frame

Four-wheel Integral drum brakes

In-line eight

THE POWER PACK

Complex for the day

The engine consists of an alloy crankcase topped by a cast-iron cylinder block and integral cylinder head. It has just one overhead cam, driven by a shaft and gears from the crankshaft and operating three valves per cylinder: two small intake ones and a single exhaust. The crankshaft runs on five roller bearings so that high oil pressure is unnecessary. The excellent power output for a 2.3-liter engine is due to the crankshaft-driven supercharger.

Three valves per cylinder

Large exhaust valves

Alloy crankcase

Crankshaft with five roller bearings

Still going

The Type 35 is one of the most prized of all classic Bugattis. Despite their enormous value, many owners still compete with their Type 35s in historic races, rallies, hill climbs and sprints. They remain highly competitive vintage racing cars.

The Type 35 is still used in competition, for which it was originally designed.

Bugatti TYPE 35

There was a Type 35 to suit everyone, from the naturally-aspirated three-bearing Type 35A through to the cars that dominated Targa Florio and the supercharged Type 35B Grand Prix winner.

Roller-bearing engine

The Type 35's crankshaft runs in roller bearings instead of plain metal, and therefore does not require high-pressure lubrication.

Outside shifter and brake lever

Inside, space is at a premium and so the shifter actually projects through the side of the cockpit through a leather gaiter. The handbrake lever is also very long to generate sufficient leverage.

Bolt-on wheel rims

The distinctive bolt-on rims were designed to prevent punctured tires from separating from the rims—a common problem with 1920s racing cars.

Offset bodywork

Type 35s are two-seaters so they can carry a riding mechanic. The unfortunate passenger has little or no protection from the wind, whereas the driver has a cowl to deflect wind away from his face.

Hollow front axle

To save weight and for improved control, the axle is hollow. It is a complicated forging.

Integral wheel and brake

The wheel is integrated with the brake drum. This means that when the wheels are removed the brake linings can be easily inspected at the same time.

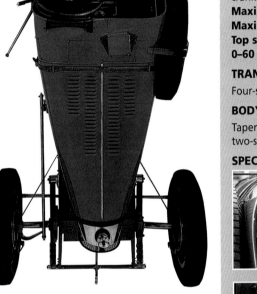

Specifications
1924 Bugatti Type 35

ENGINE
Type: In-line eight-cylinder
Construction: Cast-iron block and head with alloy crankcase
Valve gear: Three valves per cylinder (two inlet, one exhaust) operated by a shaft-driven overhead camshaft via rockers
Bore and stroke: 2.36 in. x 3.93 in.
Displacement: 2,262 cc
Compression ratio: Not quoted
Induction system: Zenith carburetor with crankshaft-driven supercharger
Maximum power: 130 bhp at 5,500 rpm
Maximum torque: Not quoted
Top speed: 125 mph
0–60 mph: 7.0 sec.

TRANSMISSION
Four-speed manual

BODY/CHASSIS
Tapered channel-section steel chassis with two-seat alloy body

SPECIAL FEATURES

The engine-turned dashboard has a full set of gauges—even a clock.

Bugatti persisted in using cable brakes so adjustment was vital.

RUNNING GEAR
Steering: Worm-and-wheel
Front suspension: Hollow axle with semi-elliptic leaf springs and friction shocks
Rear suspension: Live axle with reversed quarter elliptic leaf springs, forward radius rods and friction shocks
Brakes: Cable-operated drums (front and rear)
Wheels: Cast-alloy with integral drums
Tires: Crossply 4.95 x 28 in.

DIMENSIONS
Length: 145.1 in.   **Width:** 52 in.
Height: 42.9 in.   **Wheelbase:** 94.5 in.
Track: 45 in. (front), 47 in. (rear)
Weight: 1,654 lbs.

Bugatti ROYALE

Called the Royale as it was intended to sell to royalty rather than ordinary people, this car was too expensive even for the wealthy and only six were built. It was a magnificent failure.

"...the chauffeur's nightmare."

"*Known as 'the chauffeur's nightmare', the sheer bulk of the Royale, because of its enormous size, causes many problems. Apart from that, the Royale is surprisingly agile for such a monster. The steering is light, but with many turns lock to lock, and although the gearshift linkage is awkward, it's easy to get the hang of. The weakest point of all is the braking system: cable-operated with no servo, it isn't up to the job of hauling the Royale's imposing mass to a stop.*"

The huge steering wheel needs much turning, while the 'crash' gearshift takes some getting used to.

1927 Ettore reveals his prototype Royale, the 4,276-cc Type 41, to selected journalists at the factory in Molsheim.

The Bugatti family, with Jean Bugatti at the wheel of a 1927 prototype.

1931 After the prototype has been fitted with a number of bodies, the first production Royale appears. Production cars have a shorter wheelbase and smaller engine. All the production cars have different bodies; the first car sold is an open roadster with no lights. The second is a cabriolet for a German doctor, the third is a limousine for Cuthbert Foster.

1932 Last of the six Royales to be built is completed. The last three are not sold before the war.

1950 Two of the unsold Royales are bought by noted racer Briggs Cunningham.

1963 First car, now with Coupe Napoleon body, is sold to the infamous Fritz Schlumpf who has the world's largest collection of Bugattis.

UNDER THE SKIN

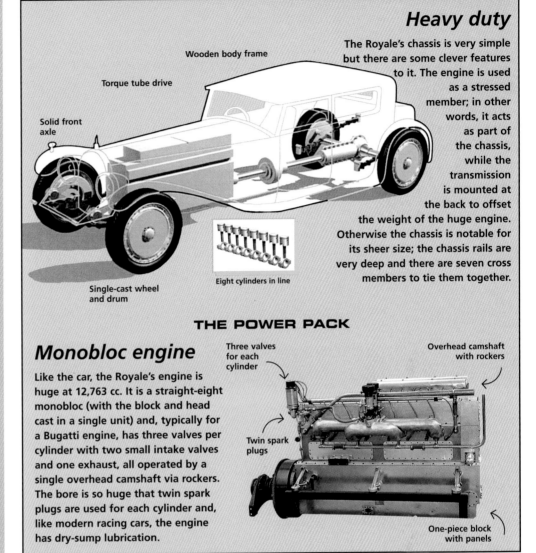

Heavy duty

The Royale's chassis is very simple but there are some clever features to it. The engine is used as a stressed member; in other words, it acts as part of the chassis, while the transmission is mounted at the back to offset the weight of the huge engine. Otherwise the chassis is notable for its sheer size; the chassis rails are very deep and there are seven cross members to tie them together.

Wooden body frame

Torque tube drive

Solid front axle

Single-cast wheel and drum

Eight cylinders in line

THE POWER PACK

Monobloc engine

Like the car, the Royale's engine is huge at 12,763 cc. It is a straight-eight monobloc (with the block and head cast in a single unit) and, typically for a Bugatti engine, has three valves per cylinder with two small intake valves and one exhaust, all operated by a single overhead camshaft via rockers. The bore is so huge that twin spark plugs are used for each cylinder and, like modern racing cars, the engine has dry-sump lubrication.

Three valves for each cylinder

Overhead camshaft with rockers

Twin spark plugs

One-piece block with panels

Near priceless

Probably some of the most expensive cars in the world, Royales have a tendency to shatter auction price records. This car's 1987 sale was upstaged by the Binder-bodied model put up for sale in 1996 by American William Lyons. The bids ended at $11,000,000!

Two-door Kellner bodywork made this Royale sell for $2,550,000 in 1987.

Bugatti ROYALE

Designed to be simply the best car in the world, the Royale was also the biggest, with the largest engine ever seen in a production car. Unfortunately it was just too big and expensive to attract even the royalty for whom it was intended.

Straight-eight engine

With a huge displacement of 12,763 cc the Royale engine produced 275 bhp. The engine was later used to power high-speed railcars for French railroads.

Live rear axle

Normal practice for pre-war cars was a live axle and the Royale is the same. Unusually, however, it is carried on reversed quarter elliptic springs rather than semi-elliptics.

Beam front axle

The Royale's front axle is a hollow forging, with two square holes cast into it, allowing the springs to pass through them.

Cast-alloy wheels

Everything about the Royale is huge, including the wheels which, at a 36-inch diameter, were the largest ever fitted to a road car. The tires had to be specially made for the Royale by Michelin.

Integral brake drums

Like Bugatti's Type 35 racing car the Royale's brake drums are integral with the wheels so that removing a wheel gives instant access to the brake.

Friction shocks

The movement of the suspension was controlled by friction shocks in the days before hydraulic shocks were available.

Three-speed transaxle

The Royale's transmission is mounted at the back to offset the weight of the huge front engine. Only three gears were necessary.

Fold-away rumble seat

This model appears to be only a two-seater but two other passengers can be carried in the rumble seat. It even has its own windshield that can be raised.

No headlights

This car is the recreation of the Royale sold to Armand Esders, a man who never drove after dark so it did not need headlights.

Specifications
1931 Bugatti Royale

ENGINE

Type: Straight-eight, overhead cam
Construction: Cast-iron monobloc with block and head cast as one
Valve gear: Three valves per cylinder (two intake, one exhaust) operated by single overhead camshaft
Bore and stroke: 4.92 in. x 5.11 in.
Displacement: 12,763 cc
Compression ratio: 6.0:1
Induction system: Single Bugatti-Schebler carburetor
Maximum power: 275 bhp at 3,000 rpm
Maximum torque: Not quoted
Top speed: 117 mph
0–60 mph: Not quoted

TRANSMISSION

Three-speed, rear-mounted transaxle

BODY/CHASSIS

Steel coachbuilt body made to order with X-braced, steel channel-section, ladder chassis

SPECIAL FEATURES

The simple fascia of the Esders roadster testifies to Bugatti's attention to quality.

The elephant mascot was designed by Ettore's sculptor brother, Rembrandt, and adopted by Ettore for the Royale.

RUNNING GEAR

Steering: Worm-and-sector
Front suspension: Solid axle with semi-elliptic leaf springs and friction shocks
Rear suspension: Live axle with reversed quarter elliptic leaf springs, additional 'helper' springs and friction shocks
Brakes: Drums front and rear, cable operated
Wheels: Alloy, 36-in. dia
Tires: Michelin 6.75 in. x 36 in.

DIMENSIONS

Length: 235 in.* **Width:** 79 in.*
Height: 64 in. **Wheelbase:** 170 in.
Track: 63 in. (front and rear)
Weight: up to 6,999 lbs.*
*varies according to model

Bugatti **TYPE 57**

With its Miller-inspired, twin-cam, straight eight, the Type 57, designed by Ettore Bugatti and his son Jean, became the most famous Bugatti road car of all time. It was available with some of the finest coachbuilt bodies.

"...a class of its own."

"It's a bit claustrophobic in the cabin of the Type 57 Atalante coupe, but a look around immediately tells you this is going to be a special drive. When new, this car must have been a revelation. The twin-cam straight eight pulls like a train, especially in supercharged form. The handling and steering were amazing for the late 1930s, and still feel great today. The cable-operated brakes on early cars aren't very reassuring, but the later hydraulic system is much better."

With its right hand driving position and smooth leather seats, the Bugatti has typical French flair.

1934 Bugatti shows the Type 57.
It is fitted with Caliber four door sedan body work.

After the rare Atlantic, the Type 57 Atalante is perhaps the most desirable model.

1935 The 57S is a short chassis,
sport version. It is introduced with a highly tuned engine.

1936 The Type 57 Series 2
is introduced. It features rubber motor mounts and a strengthened chassis.

The Type 57S had a shortened and lowered chassis.

1937 Bugatti combines
the super-charged engine of the 57C with the 57S chassis to create the fast, and very desirable 57SC.

1938 Hydraulic brakes
are available in the new series 3.

1940 Production of the
Type 57 comes to an end.

UNDER THE SKIN

Coachbuilt bodywork

Engine and transmission mount in unit

Beam front axle

Twin-cam straight-eight

THE POWER PACK

Bugatti's best

The Type 57's chassis has two deep box-section side members forming its basic structure. The engine also contributes to the structure's stiffness. When the low 57S chassis was introduced, the chassis was modified to allow the live rear axle to run through the side members. Initially, the car had cable-operated brake, but they were changed to a hydraulic system in 1938.

Miller-inspired

The original Type 57 was powered by a straight-eight twin-cam that was inspired by the work of Harry Miller. Bugatti adopted it for his own engines. The two valves (rather than the three of earlier Bugatti engines) per cylinder are operated with rocker arms and are angled at 90 degrees to one another. The engine is an all-alloy monobloc design with a six-bearing crankshaft. The basic single-carburetor engine produces 140 bhp at 4,800 rpm; with a Roots-type super-charger it could give 200 bhp.

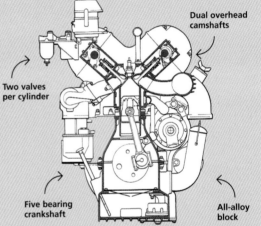

Dual overhead camshafts

Two valves per cylinder

Five bearing crankshaft

All-alloy block

Heavenly bodies

Bugatti listed various body-styles, which were then sub-contracted to nearby coach-builder Gangloff. One of the most desirable of these 'in-house' bodies is the Atalante coupe. This striking design's small cabin seems to emphasize the exclusive nature of the car.

The Atalante coupe was the best of the factory bodies.

Bugatti TYPE 57

Regarded by many as one of the greatest sports cars ever produced, the Bugatti Type 57 could outhandle and outperform almost anything else on the road except, perhaps, the Alfa Romeo 8C 2900.

Monobloc engine design

To avoid blowing a head gasket, the engine block and head were cast in one unit. This made valve adjustment a very awkward affair.

Straight-eight twin-cam

By the time the Type 57 was launched, the traditional single overhead-cam, three-valves-per-cylinder Bugatti layout had been discarded in favor of a twin-cam arrangement, inspired by the engines of designer Harry Miller.

Live rear axle

All Bugattis had live rear axles and all featured reversed quarter-elliptic leaf springs, with the end of the spring attached to the rear crossmember.

Four-speed transmission

Power is fed to the rear wheels with a four-speed transmission mounted in unit with the straight-eight engine (a Bugatti first). Fourth gear is a direct 1:1 ratio.

Coupe bodywork

The Type 57 was available with a variety of coachbuilt bodies. This Atalante coupe has a Bugatti body produced by its contracted coachbuilders, Gangloff.

Side-opening hood

Access to both sides of the engine is made easier by a side-opening hood hinged in the middle, so that either engine cover can be raised.

Specifications
1937 Bugatti Type 57 Atalante

ENGINE

Type: In-line eight-cylinder
Construction: Alloy monobloc
Valve gear: Two valves per cylinder operated by twin gear-driven overhead camshafts with rocker arms
Bore and stroke: 2.83 in. x 3.94 in.
Displacement: 3,257 cc
Compression ratio: 6.0:1
Induction system: Single Zenith updraft carburetor
Maximum power: 140 bhp at 48 rpm
Maximum torque: Not quoted
Top speed: 120 mph
0–60 mph: 10.0 sec

TRANSMISSION

Four-speed manual

BODY/CHASSIS

Ladder-type steel chassis with two-door coupe body

SPECIAL FEATURES

A small hatch behind the door provides access to extra cargo.

A small split window was a common feature of late-1930s coupes.

RUNNING GEAR

Steering: Worm-and-wheel
Front suspension: Beam axle with semi-elliptic leaf springs and Hartford Telecontrol shock absorbers
Rear suspension: Live axle with reversed quarter-elliptic springs and Hartford Telecontrol shock absorbers
Brakes: Drums (front and rear)
Wheels: Knock-on steel discs, 18-in. dia.
Tires: Crossply, 5.5 x 18 in.

DIMENSIONS

Length: 159.0 in.   **Width:** 64.0 in.
Height: 52.0 in.   **Wheelbase:** 130.0 in.
Track: 53.1 in. (front and rear)
Weight: 2,127 lbs.

Chrysler **AIRFLOW**

The Airflow was one of the most revolutionary and adventurous American cars of the 1930s, an extraordinary study of aerodynamic lines and novel packaging. It was a brilliant car, but too revolutionary for the masses of mainstream buyers.

"...inspires confidence."

"Press the gas pedal and the straight-eight rumbles willingly ahead of you. There is power to take it above 80 mph if you want, but it's better to enjoy the unbelievable amount of torque at your disposal and sit back at a gentle cruise of around 72 mph. In traffic it is tractable, and the view from the high driving position inspires confidence. The hydraulic brakes are surprisingly good and the worm-and-roller steering is remarkably accurate."

The Airflow has comfortable bench seats and an unusual instrument panel.

Milestones

1934 The wind tunnel-tested
Airflow range receives straight-eight power, a choice of four wheelbases and various bodystyles. There are three lines—Standard, Imperial and Imperial Custom. It sets speed records and wins the Monte Carlo Concours d'Elegance for design.

Chrysler Airflows are all powered by straight-eight engines.

1935 The 298-cubic inch
engine is dropped. The famous waterfall grill is replaced by a curious 'skyscraper' design.

Chrysler also offered a more conventional Airstream model.

1936 The flowing rear
end is toned down with the addition of a built-in trunk. Only one engine (a 323-cubic inch) is now offered.

1937 In the final year
of production the range reduced to just two models, and sales dwindle to 4,600 cars.

UNDER THE SKIN

Tubular-steel frame

Rear-wheel drive

Hydraulically-operated drum brakes all around

Cast-iron straight-eight

Ahead of its time

It is not only its striking bodywork—the Airflow is advanced under the skin too. The structural concept of a steel cage and network of girders and trusses onto which the body panels fitted followed aircraft principles for strength and light weight and resembles a modern-day 'safety cell,' All models are fitted with a ride stabilizer bar and the front end has longer and softer front springs. The Airflow's brakes are hydraulically operated, whereas most cars of the era still used rod or cable systems.

THE POWER PACK

Straight-eight power

Chrysler used its range of straight-eight engines in the Airflow series. Carburetion was by Ball & Ball or dual Stromberg downdrafts with automatic choke and an integral air cleaner. During its first year of production there were three engine sizes—298-, 323- and 384-cubic inches—but the 298 was dropped after the first year and the 384 was not available after 1935. Airflows sold under the De Soto badge are fitted with straight-six engines instead of eights.

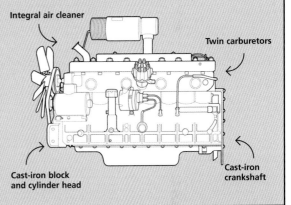

Integral air cleaner

Twin carburetors

Cast-iron block and cylinder head

Cast-iron crankshaft

1934 Imperial

The most stylish Airflow is the imposing long-wheelbase Imperial Custom —the 145-inch wheelbase best suits the car's aerodynamic lines. The most desirable model is the first year 1934, with its classic waterfall grill and sloping tail.

Airflow Custom Imperials from 1934 are highly sought after today.

Chrysler **AIRFLOW**

The Airflow was supposed to represent the future, but like so many advanced ideas the public was skeptical of this strange-looking new car, even though it offered new levels of comfort, space and driveability.

Straight-eight power

The straight-eight engine has a healthy power output and masses of torque. In addition, the unit is positioned directly over the front axle, making the hood quite short for a car of this period and allowing more room for passengers.

Aircraft-type construction

The method of construction was inspired by aviatio principles. The boc is mounted on ste beams and trusses in a similar way to contemporary aircraft's.

Advanced transmission

The three-speed manual transmission is renowned for its silent operation. It is fitted with helical gears and later examples gained a hypoid rear axle. Above 45 mph, when you lift your foot off the accelerator, overdrive is automatically engaged.

Wind-tunnel-honed body

The Airflow was one of the first cars to be tested in a wind tunnel. The aerodynamic lines helped a 1934 Imperial coupe to complete the flying mile at the Bonneville Salt Flats at 95.6 mph.

Bold nose

The front end of the 1934 model features an amazing 'waterfall' grill, 'shaped by the wind' badging and triple bumper strips. The faired in headlights look curiously like bug eyes, especially on later cars.

A glazing world first

Although most Airflows, like this one, have split windshields, some later-model Imperials boasted a new curved glass design

Puncture-proof tires

By 1936 all Airflows were fitted with new Lifeguard tires with special heavy-duty tubes and a second 'floating' tube inside.

Specifications
1934 Chrysler Airflow Sedan

ENGINE

Type: In-line eight-cylinder
Construction: Cast-iron block and head
Valve gear: Two sidevalves per cylinder
Bore and stroke: 3.25 in. x 4.50 in.
Displacement: 298 c.i.
Compression ratio: Not quoted
Induction system: Two carburetors
Maximum power: 122 bhp at 3,400 rpm
Maximum torque: Not quoted
Top speed: 88 mph
0–60 mph: 19.5 sec.

TRANSMISSION

Three-speed manual

BODY/CHASSIS

Steel girder chassis with four-door steel sedan body

SPECIAL FEATURES

The rear wheel skirts are evocative of the 1930s art deco era.

The rigorously curved surfaces of the Airflow, shaped by Oliver Clark, were unique for 1930s design.

RUNNING GEAR

Steering: worm-and-roller
Front suspension: Beam axle with leaf springs and shock absorbers
Rear suspension: Rigid axle with leaf springs and shock absorbers
Brakes: Drums (front and rear)
Wheels: Steel, 16-in. dia.
Tires: Crossply, 16-in. dia.

DIMENSIONS

Length: 235.0 in. **Width:** 77.9 in.
Height: 68.9 in. **Wheelbase:** 146.5 in.
Track: 63.0 in. (front), 61.1 in. (rear)
Weight: 4,166 lbs.

Cord **810/812**

The original Cord 810 was a revolutionary design with an advanced front-wheel drive layout and V8 power. Its performance was transformed when a supercharger was added to form the 190-bhp Cord 812.

"...outstanding performance."

"The supercharged V8 produces huge torque and once you've adjusted to the vague gearshifter, the Cord's outstanding performance can really be exploited. With front-wheel drive, steering is heavy at low speeds, although it becomes lighter as the car gains momentum. Cornering is almost neutral compared to rear-drive equivalents. The unique suspension design gives a choppy ride but the result is very little body roll for such a big, heavy car."

An aluminum instrument panel and white- faced gauges are sporty for the 1930s.

1935 Built in record time, the first Cord 810 exhibited at the New York Motor Show and immediately attracts potential customers.

The 1937 812 evolved from the 1936 810.

1936 Cord 810 production begins in sedan and convertible versions. It not as fast as it looks, with 0-60 mph taking 20.0 seconds with a top speed of 90 mph.

The 812 body tooling was bought by Graham and used for its rear-drive 1940 Hollywood sedan.

1937 To increase sales, Cord introduces the supercharged 812. It is basically the same as the 810 apart from the addition of a Schwitzer-Cummins supercharger that produces more power (170/190 bhp) and greater performance. More than seconds are trimmed off of the non-supercharged version. The more expensive Custom Cordis also introduced this year.

UNDER THE SKIN

Welded steel box-section chassis

Drum brakes front and rear

Front-wheel drive

Supercharged V8

Ahead of its time

The 812's structure was surprisingly modern, with a welded sheet-metal platform and cowl section, but with box-section side rails running from the rear wheel arches forward through the cowl to hold the engine, transmission and front suspension. It also had holes in the rails where the front driveshafts go through. Because it is a front-wheel drive layout, the 812 has trailing arms at the front and a light beam axle with semi-elliptic leaf springs at the rear.

THE POWER PACK

Airplane inspiration

Engines for the Cord were made by another Auburn-Cord-Duesenberg subsidiary, the airplane engine manufacturer Lycoming. For the 812, a modified version of the 288.6-cubic inch V8 fitted in the 810 was used. Using an iron block and alloy head design with side valves in L-heads actuated by a single camshaft, the big V8 was fitted with a Schwitzer-Cummins centrifugal supercharger. It is driven by gears at the end of the camshaft, which also drives epicyclic gears at 24 times the cam speed inside the supercharger itself. Advertised power output was 170/190 bhp—more than 40 more bhp then the standard model.

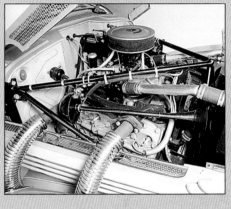

Open road

The sedan versions may be very stylish, but the most flamboyant and collectable Cord 812s are the convertible versions—the Phaeton and Sportsman. These look more stylish and sporty and, not surprisingly, command higher prices.

Externally, the Phaeton and Sportsman cabriolet are nearly identical.

Cord 810/812

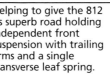

The Cord 812 was styled by one of the great car designers, Gordon Buehrig. It was like no other car on the road, thanks to its coffin-like nose, unique radiator grill and pop-up headlights.

V8 engine

Lycoming's V8 is very strong yet relatively light thanks to its alloy cylinder heads. The valve-train is a unique design with upright rockers pivoted below the camshaft actuating the valves mounted in the block and angled at 35 degrees.

Independent front suspension

Helping to give the 812 its superb road holding independent front suspension with trailing arms and a single transverse leaf spring.

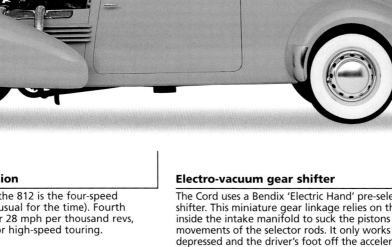

Four-speed transmission

An advanced feature of the 812 is the four-speed manual transmission (unusual for the time). Fourth gear is very tall with over 28 mph per thousand revs, making the Cord ideal for high-speed touring.

Electro-vacuum gear shifter

The Cord uses a Bendix 'Electric Hand' pre-selector gear shifter. This miniature gear linkage relies on the vacuum inside the intake manifold to suck the pistons controlling the movements of the selector rods. It only works with the clutch depressed and the driver's foot off the accelerator.

Drum brakes

Massive 12-inch, hydraulic, centrifuse drums are used on all four wheels.

Pop-up lights

Ordinary round headlights would have spoiled the Cord's bold styling and obstructed airflow, so they were designed to be concealed. In fact, the lights are basically landing light units from Stinson aircraft (also owned by Auburn-Cord-Duesenberg).

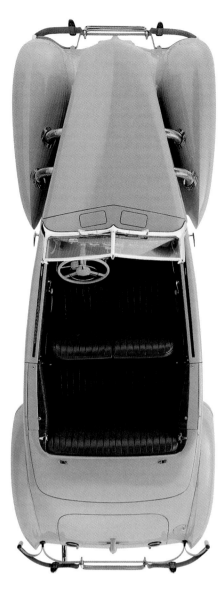

Specifications
1937 Cord 812 Supercharged

ENGINE

Type: V8
Construction: Cast-iron block and alloy cylinder heads
Valve gear: Two in-line side valves per cylinder operated by a single block-mounted camshaft with rocker arms and rollers
Bore and stroke: 3.50 in. x 3.75 in.
Displacement: 288.6 c.i.
Compression ratio: 6.3:1
Induction system: Single carburetor with mechanically driven Schwitzer-Cummins supercharger
Maximum power: 190 bhp at 4,200 rpm
Maximum torque: 272 lb-ft at 3,000 rpm
Top speed: 111 mph
0–60 mph: 13.8 sec.

TRANSMISSION

Four-speed manual

BODY/CHASSIS

Welded steel floorpan and side rails with two-door convertible body

SPECIAL FEATURES

Phaetons only differ stylistically from cabriolets by having a rear seat and quarter windows.

A crank mounted on the passenger side of the dash is used to raise and lower the headlights.

RUNNING GEAR

Steering: Gemmer centerpoint
Front suspension: Independent with trailing arms, transverse semi-elliptic leaf spring and friction shock absorbers
Rear suspension: Beam axle with semi-elliptic leaf springs and friction shock absorbers
Brakes: Hydraulically operated drums, 12-in. dia.
Wheels: 16 in. Stamped Steel, 16-in. dia.
Tires: 6.50 x 16

DIMENSIONS AND WEIGHT

Length: 195.5 in.   **Width:** 71.0 in.
Height: 58.0 in.   **Wheelbase:** 132.0 in.
Track: 55.9 in. (front), 60.9 in. (rear)
Weight: 4,110 lbs.

Delahaye **135**

The Delahaye 135 could be anything you wanted, from a strong and rugged Monte Carlo Rally and Le Mans-winning racing car to one of the most elegant coachbuilt Grand Tourers of the 1930s.

"...torquey, straight-six engine."

"It's a shock to see the tiny toy-like gear shifter in its miniature gate to the left of the steering wheel but it's no joke. You have to make sure the other, larger shifter for forward or reverse is in the right place. Then when you're moving you can zip up and down the gears at great speed without needing to use the clutch. With the torquey, straight-six engine, the performance is excellent for the period with 50 mph coming in 10 seconds."

A stylishly simple French dashboard confronts the driver of a Delahaye 135. A sprung steering wheel was typical in sports cars of the period.

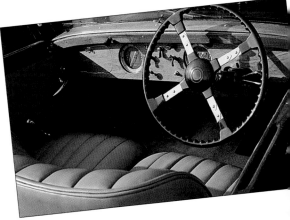

Milestones

935 The existing Delahaye Coupe des Alpes model is turned into the 135 with a lowered chassis and the existing 3.2-liter engine.

his Carlton bodywork is less lamorous than most.

936 Racing Delahaye 35s finish 2-3-4-5-7-11-12 in e French Sports Car Grand Prix t Monthlhery.

937 Cotal electrically ontrolled epicyclic transmission ecomes available and a 135 ins the Monte Carlo Rally.

938 Outlasting nuch faster cars, a 135 ins the 24 Hours of Le Mans.

948 After roducing the 135M nd the 130-bhp 135MS after the ar, Delahaye starts to introduce 35 derivatives such as the 175 nd 180 and then the 235 in 951 before production ends in 952.

his rather upright convertible 35M is bodied by Vanden Plas.

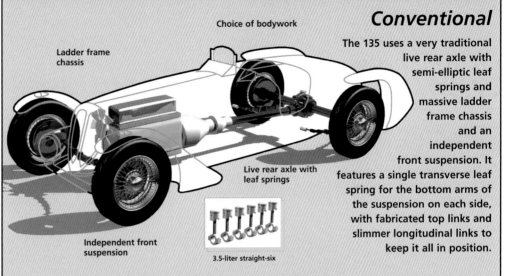

Choice of bodywork

Ladder frame chassis

Live rear axle with leaf springs

Independent front suspension

3.5-liter straight-six

Conventional

The 135 uses a very traditional live rear axle with semi-elliptic leaf springs and massive ladder frame chassis and an independent front suspension. It features a single transverse leaf spring for the bottom arms of the suspension on each side, with fabricated top links and slimmer longitudinal links to keep it all in position.

THE POWER PACK

High RPM

As simple as the chassis, the 135's engine is a very conventional overhead-valve straight-six with cast-iron block and cylinder head. It is strikingly similar to a Delahaye truck engine but has an unusually short stroke for the era so it can rev reasonably well before piston speed becomes a problem. Not surprisingly, given its truck origins, it is extremely strong but it also responds well to tuning, particularly when fitted with triple carburetors.

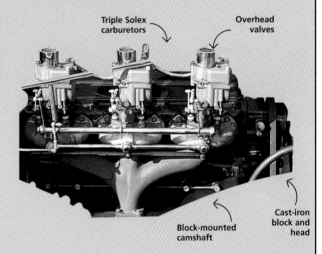

Triple Solex carburetors

Overhead valves

Block-mounted camshaft

Cast-iron block and head

Stripped down

With their stripped-down bodywork and streamlined fenders the Competition models could exceed 112 mph and handled well. They're so popular that many of the more ordinary 135s have been converted into Competition model replicas.

Many 135 Competition models have been created from sedans.

Delahaye 135

Few Delahaye 135s were as outrageous as this example, which has some of the Paris coachbuilders Figoni & Falaschi's most extravagant bodywork in 1930s' style used on the 135's simple chassis.

Narrow track

This 135 looks as though it has a particularly narrow track but that's because the wings stick out so far in order to allow the front wheels to turn.

Six-cylinder engine

The six-cylinder engine used by Delahaye is not nearly as exotic as its bodywork. It is an ordinary in-line cast-iron overhead-valve six, but it is powerful, reliable and easily tuned.

Removable fender skirts

With this type of design the all-enveloping fenders have removable sections to allow the wheels to be changed. Enclosing the wheels theoretically makes the cars more aerodynamic but it was really only a styling feature.

Cotal transmission

The expensive and complicated electrically controlled Cotal epicyclic transmission allows very fast clutchless gear shifts to be made.

Live rear axle

Delahaye kept the rear suspension design simple, with a live axle mounted on top of two semi-elliptic leaf springs along with transversely mounted adjustable shock absorbers.

Design hallmarks

One of Figoni & Falaschi's hallmarks is the way they finished off the point of the rear fenders with a chrome-encased light on each one.

Independent front suspension

Delahaye proved that an excellent design of independent front suspension could be created using a simple transverse leaf spring.

Hinged windshield

It may not look like it, but this windshield can be folded flat if the driver desires.

Specifications
1938 Delahaye 135M

ENGINE
Type: In-line six cylinder
Construction: Cast-iron block and head
Valve gear: Two valves per cylinder operated by single block-mounted camshaft, pushrods and rocker arms
Bore and stroke: 3.31 in. x 2.95 in.
Displacement: 3,557 cc
Induction system: Three Solex Type 40 carburetors
Maximum power: 110 bhp at 3,850 rpm
Maximum torque: 150 lb-ft (approx.)
Top speed: 105 mph
0–60 mph: 14.0 sec.

TRANSMISSION
Electromagnetic Cotal four-speed

BODY/CHASSIS
Steel ladder chassis frame with choice of coachbuilt bodywork

SPECIAL FEATURES

In the Cotal transmission, electromagnets change the gears according to the position of this miniature shifter. The driver only needs to use the clutch when moving away from a stop.

The Figoni & Falaschi-bodied Delahaye 135 is one of the most elegant and striking cars of the stylish 1930s.

RUNNING GEAR
Steering: Worm-and-nut
Front suspension: Transverse leaf spring with upper transverse and longitudinal links and adjustable friction shocks
Rear suspension: Live axle with semi-elliptic leaf springs and adjustable friction shocks
Brakes: Bendix drums all around
Wheels: Wire spoke 17-in. dia.
Tires: Crossply, 6 x 17 in.

DIMENSIONS
Length: 153.5 in.   **Width:** 60.9 in.
Height: 50 in.   **Wheelbase:** 87.9 in.
Track: 49.29 in. (front), 48.8 in. (rear)
Weight: 2,072 lbs.

USA 1928–1937

Duesenberg MODEL J

One of the greatest of all prewar luxury cars was built not in Europe, but in the U.S. The mighty Duesenberg Model J has a straight-eight engine with twin overhead camshafts, four valves per cylinder, and 265 bhp.

"...as though on rails."

"Unlike a Rolls-Royce, the Duesenberg was a sporty luxury car intended for keen drivers. The twin-overhead-cam, 32-valve straight-eight was basically a racing car engine that would easily rocket the Model J past 100 mph. The handling and roadholding are superior for a 1930s car, and live up to the Duesenberg catch phrase that the car takes curves 'as though on rails.' It's a big heavy car that needs a strong person behind the wheel to get the best from it."

The seat of the stars. The Duesenberg Model J was a favorite of 1930s film stars like Clark Gable and Gary Cooper.

21 The Duesenberg ompany, run by brothers ed and August, build their first oduction car, the Model A. It is e first straight-eight-engined built in the U.S.

esenbergs often carried unning bodywork.

926 Duesenberg is ken over by Errett bban Cord, who eventually vns the Auburn, Cord and uesenberg companies.

928 Duesenberg's asterpiece, the Model is launched in December.

932 Despite the all Street Crash, uesenberg introduces the odel SJ.

uesenberg brothers, Fred and ugust, founded the company.

937 The Auburn/ ord/Duesenberg roup goes out of business. uesenberg is later bought up nd its new owners stop car roduction after 436 Model Js nd 36 SJs have been made.

UNDER THE SKIN

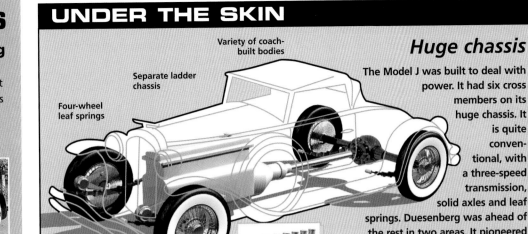

Variety of coach-built bodies

Separate ladder chassis

Four-wheel leaf springs

Hydraulic brakes

32-valve straight-eight

Huge chassis

The Model J was built to deal with power. It had six cross members on its huge chassis. It is quite conventional, with a three-speed transmission, solid axles and leaf springs. Duesenberg was ahead of the rest in two areas. It pioneered hydraulic brakes in the 1920s (the Model J's are very efficient) and the car also has the first mechanical onboard computer.

THE POWER PACK

Hi-tech straight-eight

Designed by Duesenberg, it was based on the company's successful racing engines in the 1920s, and built by Lycoming. The straight-eight engine's specification sounds modern even now, with twin cams and four valves per cylinder. It even has a mercury-filled crankshaft damper for the very long crankshaft. Only the low compression ratio (5.2:1) and very long stroke seem old fashioned. It is strong enough to be supercharged, boosting power to 320 bhp.

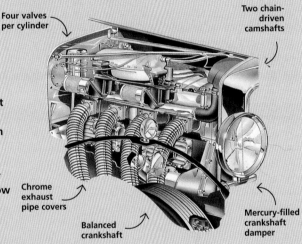

Four valves per cylinder

Two chain-driven camshafts

Chrome exhaust pipe covers

Balanced crankshaft

Mercury-filled crankshaft damper

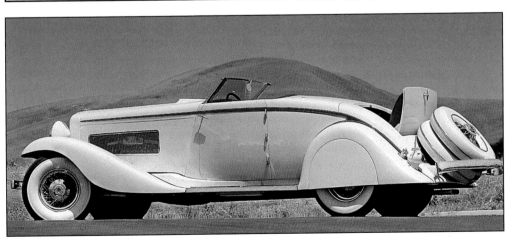

Supercharged

If a Model J was not enough you could, like Clark Gable, have the supercharged SJ. It had a centrifugal supercharger running at six times engine speed that boosted power by 55 bhp more than the standard car. Just 36 SJs were built.

Film stars Clark Gable and Gary Cooper had supercharged Duesenberg SJs.

Duesenberg MODEL J

Duesenberg was the only American automaker to win a Grand Prix and put that experience to good use in building racing-inspired engines to power cars like the Model J.

Solid front axle

Though the Duesenberg brothers were fantastic engineers, they still had no problems about using a solid front axle.

Swivelling spotlights

An intriguing feature on the Model J are the spotlights that turn along with the steering wheel so the lights follow the direction of the car.

Bodies made to order

Customers could choose to have any body they liked fitted to the Model J. Coachbuilders like Le Baron, Rollston, and Weymann built bodies to complement Duesenberg's own offerings. This model is a LeGrande convertible.

Straight-eight engine

It's an impressive technical feat to make a twin-cam straight-eight. The camshafts and crankshaft are very long and need to be well supported.

Hydraulic brakes

Duesenberg pioneered hydraulic brakes in motor racing, so it's no surprise that the Model J has huge 15-inch hydraulic drum brakes.

Luggage trunk

The rear luggage compartment was nothing more than a trunk strapped to the rear of the car.

Single stop light

In the late-1920s, it was not compulsory to have two brake lights, but this Duesenberg's single huge white stop light is still very unusual.

Specifications
1929 Duesenberg Model J

ENGINE

Type: Straight-eight twin cam
Construction: Cast-iron block and head
Valve gear: Four valves per cylinder operated by two chain-driven overhead camshafts
Bore and stroke: 3.74 in. x 4.76 in.
Displacement: 420 c.i.
Compression ratio: 5.2:1
Induction system: Single updraft Schebler carburetor
Maximum power: 265 bhp at 4,250 rpm
Top speed: 116 mph
0–60 mph: 11.0 sec. approx.

TRANSMISSION

Three-speed manual

BODY/CHASSIS

Wide choice of coachbuilt bodies on steel ladder chassis.

SPECIAL FEATURES

The Model J has a clockwork mechanism that controls the automatic chassis lubrication and the warning lights which tell the driver to change the oil.

The flamboyant chrome flexible exhaust pipes are actually decorative covers over conventional pipes.

RUNNING GEAR

Steering: Cam-and-lever
Front suspension: Solid axle with semi-elliptic leaf springs and friction shocks
Rear suspension: Live axle with semi-elliptic leaf springs and friction shocks
Brakes: Hydraulically operated drums all round, 15 in. dia.
Wheels: Wire spoked, 9 in. x 16 in.
Tires: 9 in. x 16 in. dia. crossply

DIMENSIONS

Length: 188 in.   **Width:** 67.9 in.
Height: 61 in.   **Wheelbase:** 142.5 in.
Track: 56 in. (front and rear)
Weight: 4,895 lbs.

Duesenberg **SJ**

The Duesenberg J was one of the world's finest motor cars, but the SJ was even more powerful and opulent. The addition of a supercharger turned it into a phenomenal performer.

"*...sense of superiority.*"

"When you enter the SJ, a sense of superiority pervades in terms of both design function and quality. It is not an obtrusive, heavy beast like so many of its contemporaries: indeed, the steering is light, accurate and full of feel. Open the throttle up and the gutsy noise from the engine and supercharger is almost overwhelming, as is the sheer speed—it is possible to top 100 mph in second gear! However, the antiquated chassis is not the equal of the engine."

The Duesenberg has an aura of quality that was only equaled by few of its peers.

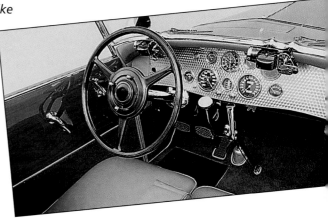

1926 Duesenberg brothers sell their car-manufacturing business to Cord.

Duesenberg was taken over by Cord when faced with the prospect of bankruptcy.

1928 An all-new Model J was announced, complete with the presupposed title of 'the world's finest car.'

The SJ uses the same engine as the J but has a supercharger.

1932 With a supercharger, the mighty SJ becomes one of the fastest road cars available. Fred Duesenburg is tragically killed behind the wheel of a SJ.

1935 A.B. Jenkins averages 135 mph on a 24-hour Bonneville run and clocks a 160-mph lap.

1937 Along with Cord and Auburn, Duesenberg is dragged down amid severe economic hardship.

Vacuum-assisted drum brakes front and rear

Tubular chassis

Leaf-sprung front and rear suspension

Inline eight engine

Being the best

Fred Duesenberg's drive for quality was evident as much under the skin as it was on the surface. Indeed, the SJ was sold as a chassis only. Massive 8-inch deep rails, plus tubular crossmembers, formed the chassis. The vacuum-assisted brakes are large and powerful and incorporate aluminum brake shoes. The same lightweight material was used for many other components.

THE POWER PACK

Supercharged superlative

A centrifugal supercharger gives the straight-eight Duesenberg engine awesome power. Even in the naturally aspirated J model, the 420-cubic inch twin-overhead camshaft engine delivers an advertised 265 bhp. The addition of a blower, with 5 psi of boost at 4,000 rpm, rockets that to an incredible 320 bhp at 4,200 rpm in stock form, with an equally impressive 425 lb-ft of torque at 2,400 rpm. Modifications required for this power output included tubular-steel con rods. With different exhaust manifolds, one engine was dyno-tested at an incredible 400 bhp, way above other engines of the 1930s.

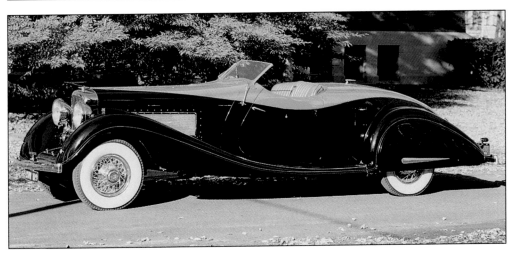

SSJ

Duesenbergs guarantee exclusivity, none more so than the two SSJ's that were specially made for Gary Cooper and Clark Gable. The 125-inch short-wheelbase cars had shattering performance. Both cars still exist as museum pieces.

Bigger and stronger than other cars, the SJ has real road presence.

Duesenberg **SJ**

With a stiffened-up engine and a blower fitted, Duesenberg's supremely accomplished Model J was transformed into the exclusive and powerful SJ. Only the extraordinarily wealthy could afford one.

Aircraft-quality engine

The undoubted centerpiece of any Duesenberg is its engine. The fabulous straight eight was extremely advanced, boasting twin overhead camshafts and four valves per cylinder. The basic engine was built by Lycoming to Fred Duesenberg's specifications.

Power brakes

The brakes were as advanced as the rest of the car's specification. With oversized shoes, braking power was impressive and was made easier by standard vacuum assistance.

Custom bodywork

In the best coachbuilt traditions, Duesenberg supplied only the chassis. Customers were expected to patronize independent coachbuilders to create whatever body-work struck their fancy. With its sporty bias, the SJ's performance suited a roadster or convertible body.

use of aluminum

s many production SJs measured more than 0 feet long, there was aturally some concern :o keep weight down. Therefore, many parts were made from aluminum, including some of the engine, lash, crankcase, water ump, intake manifold, brake shoes and gas tank.

Snaking pipes

One of the hallmarks of the SJ is its dramatic and beautifully plated exhaust headers emerging from the side of the engine. However, elaborate pipework like this does not necessarily mean the car is an SJ—the ordinary Model J was often fitted with such plumbing, even if there wasn't a supercharger.

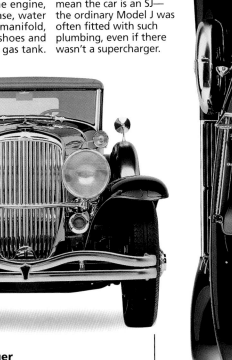

upercharger

A centrifugal blower was added to the traight eight to deliver crushing erformance on a mildly higher ompression ratio. Power shot up to 320 hp, making it easily the most powerful uto production engine in the world.

Specifications
Duesenberg SJ

ENGINE

Type: Inline eight
Construction: Cast-iron cylinder block and head
Valve gear: Four valves per cylinder operated by double chain-driven camshafts
Bore and stroke: 3.70 in. x 4.50 in.
Displacement: 420 c.i.
Compression ratio: 5.7:1
Induction system: Single Schebler carburetor plus supercharger
Maximum power: 320 bhp at 4,200 rpm
Maximum torque: 425 lb-ft at 2,400 rpm
Top speed: 130 mph
0–60 mph: 8.5 sec.

TRANSMISSION

Three-speed manual

BODY/CHASSIS

Separate chassis with convertible bodywork

SPECIAL FEATURES

A fold out rumble is available to fit two additional passengers.

As part of the effort to reduce weight, even the dashboard is aluminum.

RUNNING GEAR

Steering: Cam-and-lever
Front suspension: Beam axle with leaf springs and shock absorbers
Rear suspension: Live axle with leaf springs and shock absorbers
Brakes: Drums (front and rear)
Wheels: Wire, 19-in. dia.
Tires: Crossply, 9 in. x 16 in.

DIMENSIONS

Length: 222.5 in.
Width: 72.0 in.
Height: 70.0 in.
Wheelbase: 142.5 in.
Track: 37.5 in. (front), 58.0 (rear)
Weight: 5,000 lbs.

Ford MODEL T

If ever a car helped the world get motoring it was the Ford Model T. Built in one piece, robust and reliable, Henry Ford's dream became a global reality. The Model T is rightly recognized by many as the world's most important car.

"…Living in the past…"

"The Model T is a vastly confusing place for anyone who drives a modern car to be. The pedal layout is baffling, you have to think constantly about which lever or pedal controls what, and even then you sometimes get it wrong. Even when you've mastered the controls, the Model T isn't a pleasant car to drive. The ride is atrocious, the steering heavy and vague and the brakes practically useless. But to decry the driving experience is missing the point. The Model T was never intended to be a good drive – it was intended to be a reliable and efficient means for as many people as possible to get from A to B."

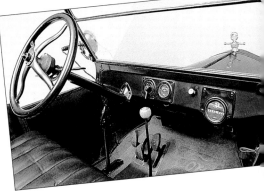

Today it might look basic, but the simple appearance disguises a very complicated layout.

1908 Ford's Model T

...oes on sale on 1 October. By the ...nd of the year, 305 examples ...ve been built.

1914 The Model T is

...mously offered by Henry Ford in ...ny colour as long as it's black", ...ue to the low cost of lead-based ...ack paint.

1915 Production

...vels exceed one million. ...ectric windscreen wipers are ...ted.

...ne of the prettiest body styles: ...Doctor's Coupé.

1919 A wish is

...nswered: Model Ts get ...n electric starter. The original ...ass finished radiator is dropped ...d replaced by a black-painted ...ckel one.

Some Model Ts, such as this one, were built in Manchester, England.

1924 The different

...odywork styles on offer are ...andardized and finished in the ...ctory. The same year, Ford ...uilds its 10 millionth Model T – a ...ur-seat roadster.

1927 With 15

...illion cars built, ...oduction of the Model T ceases ...d the all-new Model A goes on ...le to replace it.

UNDER THE SKIN

Unbreakable

The running gear is of very simple construction, with a direct gear linkage and a single propshaft to the rear axle. The axles are attached to two subframes, which are bolted to the chassis. The engine is mounted in the middle of the front subframe and sits low in the body, with a side-hinged bonnet for easy access should it need repairs or maintenance. The front bulkhead is fixed in place, meaning that owners had to build the bodywork from the rear in whatever style they chose.

Many body styles

Robust front end and chassis

Four-cylinder motor with direct linkage

2.9-liter, four-cylinder in-line engine

THE POWER PACK

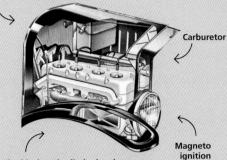

Slats in the bonnet allowed the engine to keep cool

Carburetor

Magneto ignition

The block and cylinder head were made from cast iron

Built for longevity

With 2.9 liters displacement, the Model T's engine is quite big considering it's only a four-cylinder. On paper, the 20bhp sounds like a poor output for such a large capacity unit, but the engine was designed to operate at low speeds and provide effortless torque. Because the unit spins so lazily, it will go on for years without wearing out, but the inbuilt low compression means it can be very difficult to start up. Thanks to the wide torque spread, only two forward and one backward gear were considered necessary.

Sporty Speedster

In 1910, a sporty version of the Model T appeared called the Speedster. With stripped-down bodywork and seating for just one occupant, it was designed primarily with racing in mind. it wasn't fast by today's standards, but the lighter weight meant performance, handling and braking were much better than a car with a standard body.

More show than go: The Speedster was an early attempt at a sports car.

Ford MODEL T

Probably the single most important technical advance in motoring history, the Model T brought car ownership to the masses. Henry Ford's vision of an integrated production line is still used in automobile factories today.

Gearbox

The Model T was nothing like a modern car. You had two forward gears, which you selected by pulling an outside lever and then pressing foot pedal, where the clutch is on modern car, in order to change gea Reverse gear was selected using th middle pedal.

Windscreen wipers

Model T drivers had to use a very rudimentary way of keeping their screens clear. Wipers didn't exist, but part of the screen could be lifted up so the driver could reach out and clean it with his hand.

Starting handle

Until an electric starter was introduced in 1919, Model T owners had to turn the engine by hand in order to get it to fire. The handle slotted in beneath the radiator grille and you had to turn on a tap to get fuel to the engine first.

Mudguards

This model features streamlined rear mudguards as it's a two-seater coupe. Saloon models had the guards integrated into the rear body, while van bodies sat over the axle to create a wheelarch. Basic and racing models had exposed wheels, but these were vulnerable to damage from road debris.

Hand throttle

The three foot pedals were for changing gear, engaging reverse and braking, with the brake where the gas pedal can be found on a modern car. To accelerate, drivers had to use a lever on the steering wheel to increase the amount of fuel entering the engine.

Quarter-elliptical leaf springs

Most contemporary cars came with semi-elliptic leaf springs as standard, but the Model T had smaller quarter-elliptic ones instead. This kept production costs to a minimum, but the trade-off was a harsh and bumpy ride quality.

Rear brakes

The right-hand foot pedal operated the cable brake, which applied itself to the front wheels only. It slowed the car down, but emergency stops were out of the question as it would heat up and fail completely. The rear brakes were more efficient and were operated with a hand lever.

Under the hood

The Model T engine was typical of its time. The 2.9-litre four-cylinder unit ran at low compression and had a realtively small output of just 20bhp, but it had enormous reserves of torque and could pull from very low speeds.

...of a Model T is a simple round barrel. It was ...er the driving seat as it was most protected from ... which explains the car's rather high driving ... owners carried a spare can of motor spirit on ...oard as fuel stations were few and far between..

Specifications

1908 Ford Model T

ENGINE
Engine: Four cylinder in-line
Construction: Cast iron block and cylinder head
Valve gear: Two valves per cylinder, mounted in block
Bore and stroke: 3.74 in. x 3.97 in.
Capacity: 2,895cc
Compression ratio: 4.5:1
Carburettor: One Holley direct unit
Power: 20bhp @ 1,800rpm
Top speed: 42mph
0–60mph: Not applicable

TRANSMISSION
Two-speed manual

BODY/CHASSIS
Chassis available in two lengths, wide range of bodies on offer.

SPECIAL FEATURES

Totally confusing: The left-hand pedal operates the forward gearbox, the middle pedal is used to select reverse and the right-hand pedal applies the brakes.

Front and rear, the Model T was equipped with quarter-elliptic leaf springs in order to cut production costs.

RUNNING GEAR
Steering: Direct linkage
Front suspension: Subframe, diagonal crosstubes, quarter-elliptic leaf springs
Rear suspension: Subframe, diagonal crosstubes, quarter-elliptic leaf springs
Brakes: Foot pedal operating cable to front, hand-operated cable linkage to rear
Wheels: Wooden, 30-spoke
Tires: 3.5 x 30 solid tyres

DIMENSIONS
Length: 140.0 in. **Width:** 66.0 in.
Height: Dependent on selected bodywork
Wheelbase: 100.5 in.
Track: 57.0 in. (front), 57.5 in. (rear)
Weight: 1475 lb. (applies to chassis and front bodywork only)

Ford MODEL A

After 19 years and more than 15 million sales, the venerable 'Tin Lizzie' gave way to a new Ford, the Model A. It was more complex and boasted twice as much power and proved hugely succcessful with the public.

"...huge improvement from the T."

"Even today, the Model A is recognized as a huge improvement over its predecessor, the Model T; the big L-head four is much more torquey and smooth. Given a good road, it is possible to wind the car all the way up to 65 mph, though it takes time to get there. Greatly improved springing, bigger tires and four-wheel mechanical brakes also make the A feel much more stable and secure than the Tin Lizzie. Moreover, refinement is not far shy of contemporary luxury cars."

The basic interior design of the Model A lasted through the 1930s.

Milestones

1927 After a remarkable 19-year production run, the Ford Model is phased out. Production stands at 15,007,033, a record which will remain unbroken until after World War II.

The Model A continued the legacy established by the versatile and popular 'Tin Lizzie.'

1927 Ford's Model A is introduced to much fanfare. Powered by a new 201 c.i. L-head four, 10 million people view the car during its first 36 hours on the market.

Replacing the A was the four-cylinder Model B.

1929 The two millionth Model A is built in July.

1931 Competition from Chevrolet and the Depression eat into sales. Production plumets amid rumors of a V8 Ford for 1932.

UNDER THE SKIN

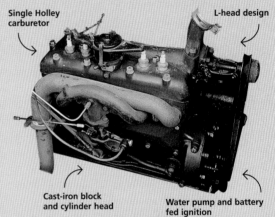

Beam axles front and rear

Four-wheel mechanically operated drum brakes

Ladder-type chassis

Big in-line four

Moving forward

Like the T, the Model A has a ladder-type steel chassis frame on to which the separate body was added. The suspension is heavily based on that of the T, with a beam axle at the front and a live rear axle with longitudinally mounted leaf springs at the rear. A new feature was four-wheel brakes. Major changes occured for 1930, including higher effort steering, and fitting 19-inch wheels in place of 21-inchers.

THE POWER PACK

All-new motor

An all-new car needs an all-new engine and that was exactly what Ford did with the Model A. A new 201-cubic inch four-cylinder L-head design, it had a cast-iron block and cylinder head. With two valves per cylinder and fuel drawn in through a single Holley carburetor, it produced 40 bhp with a 4.22:1 compression ratio—20 more than the previous Model T engine—and was far more torquey, due to a much longer 4.25 inch stroke. It was the first Ford engine to have a battery-fed ignition.

Single Holley carburetor

L-head design

Cast-iron block and cylinder head

Water pump and battery fed ignition

Open-top

During its four-year life, the Model A was an undisputed best seller, so there are still a sizeable number around. Although not the most popular when new, Roadsters and Cabriolets are the most collected of these due to their sportier looks.

Back in 1930, a Cabriolet would set you back the princely sum of $645.

Ford MODEL A

A huge gamble for the company, the Ford Model A nevertheless proved to be a hit, and its basic engineering was so sound that its legacy lived on in Ford cars built through 1948.

Big four-cylinder engine

Big displacement four-cylinder engines were common in the 1920s, offering good low end power. The Model A's 201-cubic inch 40 bhp enabled 0–60 mph times of just over 30 seconds.

Four-wheel brakes

More complex than the T, the Model introduced a few features worthy of merit. One such was four-wheel brake still mechanically operated, while 19-inch wheels were used instead of 21-inch wheels from 1930, resulting ir greater safety and an improved ride.

Adjustable windshield

Like Roadsters, Phaetons had a windshield that could be lowered by hinging it forward to rest on the ho This feature lasted until 1937, when fixed pillars were standardized.

Phaeton body

Model As were offered with a variety of different bodies. The cheapest in 1930 was the two-seat roadster priced at $435 and followed by the four-door convertible phaeton at $440. The most popular Model A body style, however, was the Tudor sedan, of which 425,124 were built.

Improved interior

1930 brought a number of noticeable changes, both inside and out. Highlighting a roomier interior was an improved dash with centrally placed instruments, including a 'cyclops eye' speedometer.

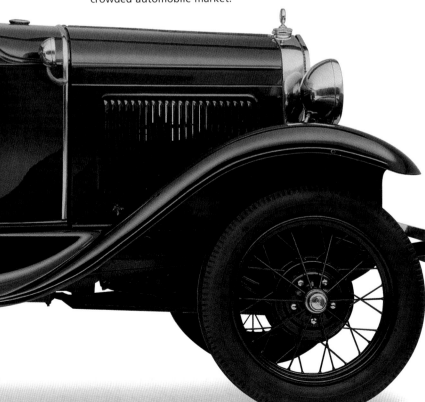

Ladder-type frame

In keeping with Henry Ford's ideas of standardization in manufacturing, all Model As rode the same 103.5-inch, fully boxed steel chassis. This also saved production time and enabled competitive pricing in an increasingly crowded automobile market.

Specifications
1930 Model A Phaeton

ENGINE

Type: In-line four

Construction: Cast-iron block and head

Valve gear: Two valves per cylinder operated by a single camshaft via pushrods

Bore and stroke: 3.88 in. x 4.25 in.

Displacement: 201 c.i.

Compression ratio: 4.22:1

Induction system: Single Holley carburetor

Maximum power: 40 bhp at 2,200 rpm

Maximum torque: 128 lb-ft at 1,000 rpm

Top speed: 65 mph

0–60 mph: 32.0 sec

TRANSMISSION

Three-speed manual

BODY/CHASSIS

Steel ladder chassis with steel Phaeton body

SPECIAL FEATURES

Turn signals are a later addition to this otherwise stock Phaeton.

The engine could still be started by turning a handle off the crankshaft.

RUNNING GEAR

Steering: Worm-and-roller

Front suspension: Beam axle with transverse leaf spring and lever arm type shock absorbers

Rear suspension: Live axle with longitudinal leaf springs and lever arm-type shock absorbers

Brakes: Drums, front and rear

Wheels: Steel, 19-in. dia.

Tires: 4.5 x 19 in.

DIMENSIONS

Length: 146.8 in. **Width:** 63.5 in.

Height: 71.6 in. **Wheelbase:** 103.5 in.

Track: 56.0 in. (front and rear)

Weight: 2,212 lbs.

Ford **DELUXE V8**

The 1939-1940 Ford V8 is regarded by many collectors as the best of the famous pre-war V8 Ford line. With up-to-the-minute styling and plenty of power, it was immensely popular with buyers, too.

"...ride in total comfort."

"Open up the door and climb in. After you take your position behind the Deluxe's wide steering wheel and start up its flat-head V8, some of the embellishments that make this a Deluxe model become evident—namely the wood-grain dash and large-faced clock. Like all upgraded models, this Deluxe has the optional 85 bhp engine. Its firm body construction and advanced (for its time) suspension give a better than average ride in total comfort."

The stylish sprung steering wheel and beautiful dash make for a classic interior.

Milestones

1932 America's first bargain-priced
V8 appears as Henry Ford boldly launches a range of eight-cylinder cars.

Fords gained fender-mounted headlights for 1938.

1933 New and widely
admired airflow designs are now on a longer 112-inch wheelbase.

1935 More engine changes
and a fuller body style enhance the V8's attractiveness.

A new grill and minor refinements distinguish the 1939 from the 1940 model.

1939 Distinctive styling
changes are made, notably to the front grill.

1942 As Ford turns over
its factories exclusively to war-time production, the V8 line is shut down.

Solid axles front and rear

Hydraulic drum brakes

Separate chassis frame

Flathead V8

Stretched frame

In 1933, the frame of the V8 was completely redesigned with a double drop and cross bracing, gaining an extra six inches in the wheelbase at the same time. As for the rest of the specification, that looks back to Model T days, with solid axles on transverse leaf springs front and rear. New for the 1939 cars were four-wheel hydraulic drum brakes. Henry Ford always believed that simpler is better.

THE POWER PACK

Ford's first V8

Henry Ford had originally considered building a radical 'X8' engine but settled on a more conventional V8 for production. This was a classic piece of engineering, a simple yet effective flat-head cast-iron unit. In its original 221-cubic inch guise, it put out 65 bhp, rising to 85 bhp in 1934 thanks to a new carburetor and intake manifold. Initial reliability problems were soon cured, and the V8 gained a reputation as one of the most durable engines around, particularly with hot rodders. After the war, the V8 would return with a larger 239-cubic inch displacement.

V8 Deluxe

The V8 has a strong and enduring reputation and will always be regarded as one of the all-time greats. The 1940 Deluxes are among the most coveted pre-war Fords, due in part to their neat Bob Gregorie styling, rugged engineering and unabashed charm. Hydraulic brakes make stopping easier, too.

1940 Deluxes have long been collectors' favorites.

Ford **DELUXE V8**

Durability and affordability were the hallmarks that established Ford, and though the V-8 boasted both of those qualities, its performance was the most impressive feature.

V8 engine

Crucial to Ford's success in the 1930s was its V8 powerplant. When other car makers had only fours and sixes, Ford could justly claim superiority with not one but two different V8 engines.

V-grill

The distinctive V-shaped grill arrived in 1935 and developed into the streamlined profile see on this 1939 Deluxe four-door sedan. The 1939 has vertical gri bars in place of the horizontal bars of the 1940 Deluxe.

Steel

Early V8 models had a fabric roof but in 1937 Ford began using steel roof

Deluxe interiors

All Deluxe models came with a woodgrain dashboard and a centrally mounted clock.

Faired-in headlights

The popular airflow look arrived for the Ford range in 1937. Apart from the chiseled front end styling, this took the form of fully faired-in, ellipsoid headlights.

Optional taillight

Only the Deluxe models came with two taillights as standard. The base models only came with one taillight. However, certain states at this time required cars to have two taillights. So some standard models had the extra taillight installed at the dealership.

Specifications
1939 Ford Deluxe V8

ENGINE

Type: V8

Construction: Cast-iron cylinder block and heads

Valve gear: Two side-mounted valves per cylinder operated by a single camshaft

Bore and stroke: 3.06 in. x 3.75 in.

Displacement: 221 c.i.

Compression ratio: 6.2:1

Induction system: Single carburetor

Maximum power: 85 bhp at 3,800 rpm

Maximum torque: 155 lb-ft at 2,200 rpm

Top speed: 87 mph

0–60 mph: 17.4 sec.

TRANSMISSION

Three-speed manual

BODY/CHASSIS

Separate chassis with steel two-door or four-door sedan, coupe or convertible body

SPECIAL FEATURES

Suicide-type rear doors were offered on four-door sedans in 1939.

Ellipsoid headlights were faired into the front fenders.

RUNNING GEAR

Steering: Worm-and-roller

Front suspension: Beam axle with transverse leaf spring and shocks

Rear suspension: Live axle with transverse leaf spring and shocks

Brakes: Drums (front and rear)

Wheels: Steel, 17-in dia.

Tires: 6 x 16 in.

DIMENSIONS

Length: 179.5 in. **Width:** 67.0 in.

Height: 68.6 in. **Wheelbase:** 112.0 in.

Track: 55.5 in. (front), 58.3 in. (rear)

Weight: 2,898 lbs.

Frazer **NASH TT REPLICA**

The most famous of all the pre-war Frazer Nash cars, the chain-driven TT Replica was archaic even in the 1930s. Nevertheless, it worked well and the TT proved a successful race and trials car.

"...a thrilling ride."

"You need the big, sprung steering wheel to cushion the severe jolts fed through the crude and stiff suspension, but with such great handling this becomes quite insignificant. The slightest movement of the steering wheel immediately translates into a turn, almost more like a motorcycle than a car. The Meadows engine is eager enough and, coupled with the surprisingly easy-to-use transmission, makes for an absolutely thrilling ride."

The extremely rudimentary cabin is for true driving enthusiasts.

Milestones

1932 Frazer Nash decides to celebrate its entries in the Tourist Trophy (or TT) races at Dundrod in Ireland with the TT Replica.

Archibald Frazer Nash started building his own cars in 1927.

1933 The first TT Replica is built with a six-cylinder Blackburne engine and has a long chassis made of thicker steel.

Frazer Nash also had controlling interest in Invicta; this is an Invicta S-type.

1934 Frazer Nash changes the chassis design by extending the siderails to the end of the car rather than just to where the rear quarter-elliptic springs are mounted.

1935 The last TT Replica is made by Frazer Nash after the company built a total of 85 cars spanning 6 years.

UNDER THE SKIN

Simple, channel rail chassis

Chain drive

Ash-framed body

Robust in-line four

Utter simplicity

The Frazer Nash cars were unusually competitive due to their light weight and simplicity. The TT chassis has two channel-section rails and very little crossbracing is needed in the very narrow car. The lightweight body is ash-framed and alloy-paneled. The suspension is very basic, with a solid axle and quarter-elliptic leaf springs in both the front and rear. Instead of a conventional transmission, the TT has sets of sprockets and chains connected to a solid rear axle.

THE POWER PACK

Meadows mill

Frazer Nash used different engines from outside suppliers such as Anzani and Blackburne but the TT Replica was most often fitted with the 1.5-liter, four-cylinder engine supplied by the Harry Meadows company. This has an iron block and alloy crankcase with a long stroke. However, a modern overhead-valve crossflow cylinder head with the twin SU carburetors sits on one side and the exhaust on the other to provide more efficient breathing. The two valves per cylinder are operated by pushrods and rockers using a single block-mounted, gear-driven camshaft. The power output of 62 bhp is enough to push the 1,848-lb. TT to 87 mph.

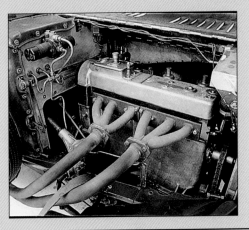

Supercharged

All TT Replicas had detail differences that made them quite desirable. The fastest of all are the 120 bhp supercharged cars. These were fast—one reached 113 mph at Brooklands—but unreliability precluded any street-legal blown TTs. Nevertheless, 62-bhp cars still deliver satisfactory performance.

Fitting a supercharger boosted power to around 120 bhp.

Fraser NASH TT REPLICA

With exposed front cycle fenders (easily detachable for racing), tall wire wheels, fold-down windshield, cutaway door and large, exposed rear fuel tank, the TT was typical for a pre-war British sports car.

Meadows engine

The in-line, 1.5-liter engine, built by Harry Meadows Ltd., was often improved on the TT Replica by fitting the Deflectorhead with revised port shapes and bigger valves. This increases turbulence in the combustion chamber and increases power output.

Solid rear axle

There is no differential in the rear axle; it is just a solid shaft that gives the TT enormous traction. This is possible because the rear track is very narrow compared with the front.

Folding windshield

To decrease the car's frontal area, which h a considerable effect on top speed, the fla windshield can be folded flat on top of the hood, leaving the driver and passenger protected from the wind by small, round windows.

Chaindrive

The axle has a sprocket with the same number of teeth as on the driveshaft, with extra sprockets to control the gearing. These could be altered to suit cruising or sprinting.

Four-speed transmission

Basically a collection of outside-mounted sprockets fitted to a transverse shaft just ahead of the rear axle, the TT's transmission is simple but very effective and proved to be reliable, too.

Exposed fuel tank

The TT Replica features a round back. Below it is a separate 12-gallon fuel tank complete with a quick-release fuel filler that was wide enough for quick refueling in competition events. Air is forced from the tank, originally by pressurized air, and there is an air-pressure gauge on the dashboard that indicates when the pressure drops and requires action from the hand pump in the cockpit.

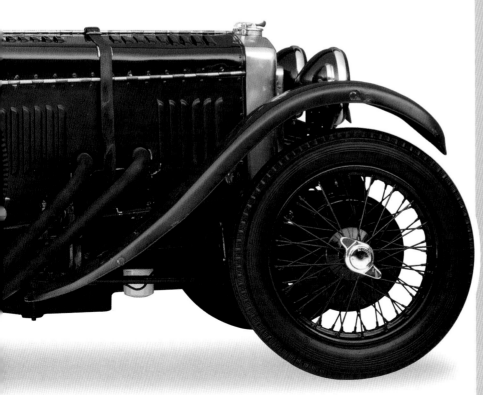

Specifications
1935 Frazer Nash TT Replica

ENGINE

Type: In-line four-cylinder
Construction: Cast-iron block and cylinder head with alloy crankcase
Valve gear: Two valves per cylinder operated by a single block-mounted gear-driven camshaft with pushrods and rockers
Bore and stroke: 2.72 in. x 3.94 in.
Displacement: 1,496 cc
Compression ratio: 10.0:1
Max power: 62 bhp at 4,500 rpm
Max torque: Not quoted
Top speed: 87 mph
0–60 mph: 18.0 sec

TRANSMISSION

Four-speed manual

BODY/CHASSIS

Separate channel-section steel ladder frame with alloy two-seater convertible body

SPECIAL FEATURES

The chaindrive and rear axle can be accessed using a lift-off panel behind the seats.

There is no door on the driver's side, as that is where the gear lever and handbrake lever are mounted.

RUNNING GEAR

Steering: Worm-and-sector
Front suspension: Tubular beam axle with reversed quarter-elliptic leaf springs, radius arms and friction shock absorbers
Rear suspension: Solid axle with quarter-elliptic leaf springs, radius arms and friction shock absorbers
Brakes: Drums, 12-in. dia. (front and rear)
Wheels: Wire spoke center-lock, 19-in. dia.
Tires: 4.50 x 19

DIMENSIONS

Length: 138.0 in.   **Width:** 40.0 in.
Height: 38.5 in.   **Wheelbase:** 102.0 in.
Track: 48.0 in. (front), 42.0 in. (rear)
Weight: 1,848 lbs.

Graham HOLLYWOOD

When Auburn-Cord-Duesenberg went out of business, two companies tried to save the incredible Cord. One was Graham-Paige, which transformed the front-wheel drive 810/812 into the rear-drive Hollywood.

"...in a class all its own."

"It may be based on the Cord 810, but the Hollywood behaves differently due to its rear-wheel drive chassis. Narrow tires and vague steering can be somewhat disconcerting at first, especially with so much power on command from the supercharged engine. The three-speed transmission is surprisingly smooth, and for cruising at high speed, the Graham is in a class all its own. A short wheelbase results in fair handling, though stopping needs care."

A stainless steel dashboard and split windshield give a typical 1940s look.

935 The Auburn Motor Co. introduces the rd 810 at the New York Show. has completely new styling d front-wheel drive.

others Joe, Robert and Ray aham started building cars 1928 as Graham-Paige.

936 Production ets underway with ur bodystyles.

937 The more owerful supercharged 2 is launched.

aham production jumped 1935, to 18,500 cars.

939 Joe Graham pproaches Norm de ux to build a version of the rd 810 using a rear-drive assis. De Vaux, owner of Cord oling, agrees and the Holly-ood goes into production in 40. It is expensive to produce d is a slow seller. Graham ds production in late 1940.

Four-wheel drum brakes

Separate steel chassis

Beam-axle front suspension

Supercharged six

A simpler way

Graham had to make significant changes to the original Cord 810 to suit a simpler, rear-drive format. This required a new front suspension with a proven but somewhat archaic beam axle suspended on leaf springs. At the rear is a solid axle mating the driveshaft to the differential. It is also located and suspended by semi-elliptic leaf springs. Like most cars of the period, braking is by four-wheel, non-adjusting drums.

THE POWER PACK

Continental engine

The original Cord 810/812 series relied on a Lycoming V8 engine, but the Graham brothers chose a different, less expensive route. In this case, it was Continental that supplied the 218-cubic inch, inline six-cylinder engine. This sidevalve design, with an iron block and alloy head, was available in normally aspirated form, producing 93 bhp (95 for 1941). Fitting Graham's own supercharger gave an extra 26 bhp (29 in 1941). Like most sidevalve engines, it had a long stroke (in this case 4.38 inches) and was designed for low-rpm torque. All the valves are on one side, operated by a single camshaft.

Hip Hup

Even rarer than the Graham Hollywood, with just 354 built, is the Hupmobile Skylark. Like the Hollywood, it was a way of keeping the look of the Cord 812 alive. It has a different engine and rear-wheel drive layout, as well as a restyled nose.

Hupmobile's Skylark looks almost identical to the Graham.

Graham HOLLYWOOD

Graham-Paige chose the four-door Beverly Sedan shape rather than the two-door convertible from the various Cord bodystyles because it was intended to make the car a popular, mass-market contender.

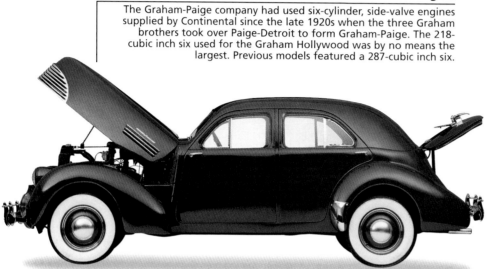

Side-valve engine

The Graham-Paige company had used six-cylinder, side-valve engines supplied by Continental since the late 1920s when the three Graham brothers took over Paige-Detroit to form Graham-Paige. The 218-cubic inch six used for the Graham Hollwood was by no means the largest. Previous models featured a 287-cubic inch six.

Pod headlights

The idea behind the Graham Hollywood was to produce a simpler, and less expensive car than the Cord. One of the complicated items to be dispensed with was the pop-up headlights. The lights were replaced by free-standing units mounted in pods on top of the fenders.

Three-speed transmission

While the Cord has a complicated remote electromagnetic-vacuum gear shifter with its own miniature gate (a system that could also be used as a pre-selector transmission), the Graham Hollywood uses a much simpler conventional manual unit. Like many Detroit cars of the time, the transmission has a column shift.

Split windshield

Technology to produce compound curved glass had not been perfected in 1940. Even Cadillacs had split windshields, and the Cord and Graham Hollywood followed suit. The design is mirrored in the back window, which is also a two-piece split unit.

Live rear axle

With a switch from front to rear drive, the Cord beam rear axle was replaced by a live unit and differential, located and sprung on semi-elliptic leaf springs like most contemporary automobiles.

Specifications
1941 Graham Hollywood

ENGINE

Type: Inline six-cylinder

Construction: Cast-iron block and alloy head

Valve gear: Two inline sidevalves per cylinder operated by a single block-mounted camshaft and solid valve lifters

Bore and stroke: 3.25 in. x 4.38 in.

Displacement: 218 c.i.

Compression ratio: 7.1:1

Induction system: Single Carter carburetor with Graham supercharger

Maximum power: 124 bhp at 4,000 rpm

Maximum torque: 182 lb-ft at 2,400 rpm

Top speed: 89 mph

0–60 mph: 14.6 sec.

TRANSMISSION

Three-speed manual

BODY/CHASSIS

Separate box-section steel frame with four-door sedan body

SPECIAL FEATURES

A split rear window is standard on all Graham Hollywoods.

In addition to fixed headlights, the Graham also has a different grill.

RUNNING GEAR

Steering: Worm-and-roller

Front suspension: Beam axle with semi-elliptic leaf springs and telescopic shock absorbers

Rear suspension: Live axle with semi-elliptic leaf springs and telescopic shock absorbers

Brakes: Drums (front and rear)

Wheels: Pressed steel discs, 5 x 16 in. dia.

Tires: Bias-ply, 6.00 x 16

DIMENSIONS

Length: 190.5 in.   **Width:** 71.0 in.

Height: 60.5 in.   **Wheelbase:** 115.0 in.

Track: 57.5 in. (front), 61.0 in. (rear)

Weight: 3,240 lbs.

Hispano-Suiza **H6B**

After World War I, Rolls-Royce's claim to building the best car in the world was hard to believe. There was a new contender produced in France with more advanced engineering and better performance—the Hispano-Suiza H6B.

"...simply outstanding."

"In 1919 driving a Hispano-Suiza H6B was like riding a magic carpet. The engine was incredibly smooth and flexible with amazing power. The servo brakes were revolutionary, with road testers bragging that it stops as though the car was being grabbed by a giant hand. Long leaf springs give a superb ride while the steering was the perfect mix of weight and directness. The acceleration and top speed were astounding for the day."

Like many cars of the era, the H6B has a right-mounted gearshift mechanism.

1919 With World War I over, Hispano-Suiza stuns the motoring world by displaying the new H6B at the Paris Motor Show. The new 6.6-liter overhead-cam-engined car is made in chassis form to be bodied by outside coachbuilders of the customer's choice.

Hispano-Suiza pioneered the use of a servo brake system.

1924 Following success in the Coupe Boillot races at Boulogne, Hispano-Suiza brings out the H6C Boulogne. Larger cylinder liners give a capacity of 7,982 cc increasing power to 150 bhp.

Following on from the H6 was the monstrous V12 Type 68.

1934 Production of the H6 finally ends. By 1931, Hispano-Suiza has launched the incredible Type 68 V12 model, but there is such loyalty to the six-cylinder car that production has to carry on for a few more years until almost 2,200 are finally built.

UNDER THE SKIN

Solid engineering

Crossmembers behind transmission

Live rear axle

Solid beam front axle with semi-elliptic leaf springs

Low-revving in-line six

Two deep channel-section rails form the sidemembers of the perimeter chassis frame and rise sharply to form at the rear over the live axle. They are joined by three substantial crossmembers behind the transmission. Suspension is non-independent; the front is a beam carried on semi-elliptic leaf springs, while the rear is a live axle, carried on semi-elliptic leafs but with a torque tube running as far as the main crossmember.

THE POWER PACK

Airplane technology

Hispano-Suiza produced superb airplane engines in World War I, and the 135-bhp, 6.6-liter, in-line six-cylinder found in the H6 was inspired by these airplane powerplants. To keep it light, the block is a simple alloy casing with screw-in steel liners for the alloy pistons to run in. Like the block, the cylinder head is also cast from alloy and features aircraft-style valve gear; a single overhead camshaft opens and closes the valves with Hispano's patented threaded-capped valve stems. In 1924, the engine was bored out to 8.0-liters and power jumped up to 150 bhp. More power was available on racing versions.

Personalized racer

Most famous of all the H6 range is the incredible H6C Boulogne built for the extremely wealthy André Dubonnet to race in 1924. It has a convertible body made of lightweight tulip wood, and as well as being a minor work of art, it is fast, too: it finished sixth in the Targa Florio. Most H6s, however, had formal sedan-type bodywork.

The H6 could be bodied according to customer preference.

Hispano-Suiza **H6B**

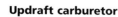

The style and appearance of the Hispano-Suiza H6B depended entirely on what sort of bodywork the customer wanted. That could range from elegant open tourers to formal closed sedans.

Updraft carburetor

For such a superbly designed engine, the breathing is still restricted. Fuel is fed through a double Solex updraft carburetor with a long pipe to one end of the intake manifold, making fuel delivery uneven to all of the cylinders. The exhaust manifold on the other side of the head is also poorly shaped.

Six-cylinder engine

Hispano-Suiza's great model H airplane engine powered the fast SPAD fighters of World War I. Most of the quality was found in its 6.6-liter six-cylinder, alloy-cased, wet-liner car engine. The valve adjustment is very clever and also follows airplane engine design.

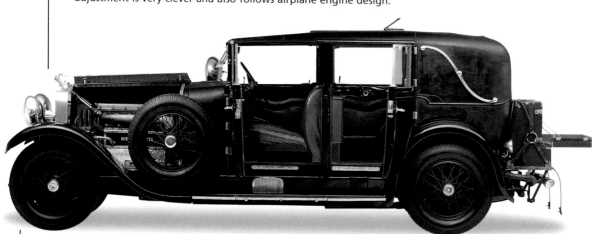

Solid front axle

The H6B has a solid-beam axle under the chassis rails. It is both suspended and located by semi-elliptic leaf springs. There is a shorter section of spring ahead of the axle to give better location.

Servo brakes

A small drum is driven off the transmission with its brake shoe attached to the brake pedal. The lining is also attached by a rod to the other brakes and as the brake is applied, the rotating drum grabs and moves the lever to the other brakes.

Wire wheels

There was no doubt that the H6B would have anything other than center-lock wire spoke wheels. They had to be large to allow room for the enormous brake drums and to give the ground clearance required in the days when roads were very poor.

Specifications
1920 Hispano-Suiza H6B

ENGINE
Type: In-line six-cylinder
Construction: Alloy crankcase with forged-steel liners and alloy head
Valve gear: Two valves per cylinder operated by a single overhead camshaft
Bore and stroke: 3.94 in. x 5.51 in.
Displacement: 6,597 cc
Compression ratio: 4.5:1
Induction system: Twin Solex carburetors
Maximum power: 135 bhp at 3,000 rpm
Maximum torque: Not quoted
Top speed: 85 mph
0–60 mph: 18.9 sec.

TRANSMISSION
Three-speed

BODY/CHASSIS
Separate channel-section steel perimeter chassis with four-door sedan body

SPECIAL FEATURES

Despite their size, the headlights are only moderately effective.

Trunk had a literal meaning back in the early 20th century.

RUNNING GEAR
Steering: Screw-and-nut
Front suspension: Beam axle with semi-elliptic leaf springs and friction shock absorbers
Rear suspension: Live axle with semi-elliptic leaf springs and torque tube; later with friction shock absorbers
Brakes: Alloy-cased drums, 15.75-in. dia. (front and rear)
Wheels: Wire spoke, 26-in. dia.
Tires: 35 x 5 in.

DIMENSIONS
Length: 192.0 in   **Width:** 73.2 in.
Height: 73.3 in.   **Wheelbase:** 146.0 in
Track: 57.0 in. (front), 57.0 in. (rear)
Weight: 4,250 lbs.

Hispano-Suiza TYPE 68

The height of luxury and technology built at the depths of the great depression, the Hispano-Suiza Type 68 with its huge V12 engine and coachbuilt body was a beautiful engineering masterpiece and an indulgence for those wealthy enough to afford one.

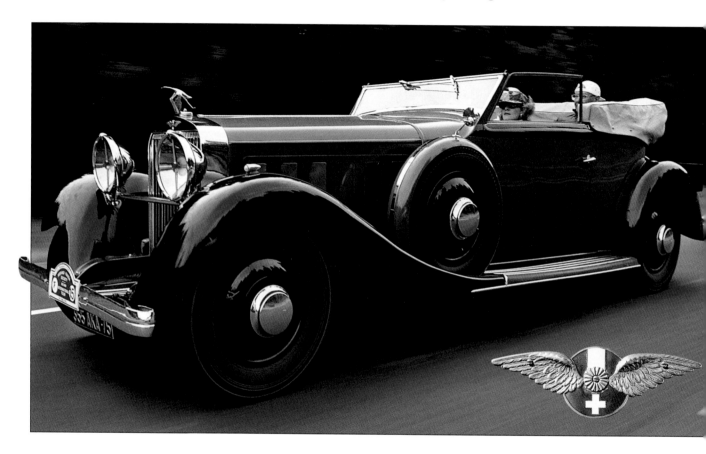

"...gives plenty of torque."

"Figures weren't quoted but the 9.5-liter V12 engine gives plenty of torque, delivered in the quiet, smooth way only a V12 can guarantee. All Type 68s had heavy coachbuilt bodies, but the V12 pulls with ease and cruises happily at 80 mph. The clutch is heavy, the three-speed gearshift firm and the ride is smooth. Although never intended to be thrown into bends, it can be cornered with a fair degree of accuracy. Unlike some of its rivals the Type 68s has servo-assisted brakes."

Luxurious interior of the Type 68 features acres of wood, leather and wool carpeting. Art-deco styling gives away the car's age.

Milestones

1931 The Type 68 is unveiled at the Paris Motor Show. To demonstrate the high quality engineering and reliability of the car, it is driven from Paris to Nice and back without needing oil or water. It is available in chassis form only. There is a choice of four chassis lengths to suit different bodywork.

Longer chassis lent themselves to limousine bodywork.

1935 As if 9.5 liters is not enough the engine's stroke is lengthened to increase the V12's displacement to 11,310 cc to form the Type 68b. The larger engine increases power by 30 bhp over the most powerful of the two 9.5-liter versions to give 250 bhp. That lowers the 0–60 mph time to 11.5 seconds.

1938 Production ceases in the company's French factory as Hispano-Suiza turned to building aero-engines.

Hispano-Suiza also built smaller six-cylinder cars.

UNDER THE SKIN

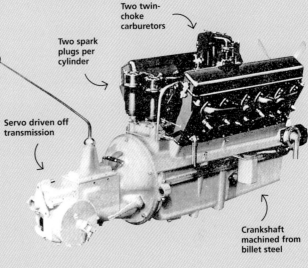

Conventional ladder chassis

Live rear axle

Servo-assisted brakes

Beam front axle

Adjustable shocks

Enormous 9.5-liter V12

Simple chassis

Hispano kept the chassis simple. It is a conventional cross-braced ladder frame, available in four wheelbases to suit different body styles. Suspension is equally simple, with a beam front axle and live rear axle both on leaf springs, although the friction shocks are fully adjustable via a control situated in the cockpit.

THE POWER PACK

Huge V12

To avoid cylinder head gasket problems the heads and block are one alloy casting. The pushrod overhead-valve V12 has two spark plugs per cylinder to improve combustion, which are mounted horizontally under the valves. The long connecting rods are hollow to keep weight down but the one-piece crankshaft was machined down to about 70 lbs. from billet steel originally weighing a massive 970 lbs. That's only 66 pounds less than the overall weight of a Caterham 7 Superlight!

Two twin-choke carburetors

Two spark plugs per cylinder

Servo driven off transmission

Crankshaft machined from billet steel

Body beautiful

The Type 68s were all bodied by outside coachbuilders and customers had the choice of the world's best companies; Saoutchik of Paris, Vanvooren, Letourneur et Marchand, Binder, Kellner, Gurney Nutting and Fernandez & Darrin.

Owners could choose from a variety of bodies from different coachbuilders.

Hispano-Suiza TYPE 68

The goal of the Type 68 was a high-speed car with the greatest possible refinement. With the optional 11-liter engine the Type 68 could haul along at more than 112 mph in perfect comfort.

Alloy V12 engine

Although the V12 engine was huge, its weight was kept down by using alloy castings and hollow connecting rods. Two compression ratios were offered, 5.0:1 and 6.0:1 giving two different power outputs: 190 and 220 bhp respectively.

Twin ignition

With twin spark plugs for each cylinder and twin magnetos to fire them, the Hispano could suffer the total failure of one ignition system and still run with no trouble.

Thermatically controlled slats

Only when the engine had reached operating temperature would a thermostat open the slats on the radiator grill allowing air to pass through it.

Four chassis options

To suit the many styles of bodywork which might be fitted to a Type 68 chassis, the factory offered four different wheelbase lengths.

Adjustable shocks

Although the shocks are the crude mechanical friction type, their stiffness could be adjusted with two controls on the steering column to alter the ride for maximum comfort or all-out handling.

Servo-assisted brakes

The Type 68 uses a mechanical servo driven by the transmission to help increase the braking force.

Fully retractable top

To keep the lines as smooth and flowing as possible the soft top on this Fernandez & Darrin design folds away completely, hidden by a flush-mounted metal cover.

Coachbuilt body

All Type 68s had coachbuilt bodies. This one is built on the second shortest available wheelbase by Fernandez & Darrin. This car was once owned by famous model and perfume mogul Coco Chanel.

Flying stork emblem

World War I French fighter ace Georges Guynemer used the stork emblem for his squadron. His planes were powered by Hispano-Suiza engines. Marc Birkigt adopted the emblem in memory of the pilot shot down and killed in 1917.

Twin exhausts

Twin exhausts were natural with a big V12 engine. In this case there were dual three-into-one exhaust manifolds on each bank of cylinders.

Specifications
1934 Hispano-Suiza Type 68

ENGINE
Type: V12
Construction: Light alloy block and heads cast together
Valve gear: Two valves per cylinder operated by single camshaft, pushrods and rockers
Bore and stroke: 3.94 in. x 3.94 in.
Displacement: 9,425 cc
Compression ratio: 5.0:1
Induction system: Two Hispano-Suiza twin-choke carburetors
Maximum power: 190 bhp at 3,000 rpm
Maximum torque: Not quoted
Top speed: 103 mph
0-50 mph: 12.0 sec.

TRANSMISSION
Three-speed manual

BODY/CHASSIS
Choice of four different length steel ladder frame chassis with cross braces. Bodywork supplied by outside coachbuilders to customer's requirements

SPECIAL FEATURES

The servo takes power to increase the pressure applied to the brakes.

The stork logo, inlaid into wooden door trim, shows off the car's luxury.

RUNNING GEAR
Steering: Worm-and-nut
Front suspension: Beam axle with semi-elliptic leaf springs and friction shocks
Rear suspension: Live axle, semi-elliptic leaf springs and friction shocks
Brakes: Drums, mechanical servo-assisted
Wheels: Wire spoke, 17-in. dia.
Tires: Michelin crossply 4.5 in. x 17 in.

DIMENSIONS
Length: 212 in.   **Width:** 71 in.
Height: 58.4 in.   **Wheelbase:** 146 in.
Track: 57 in. (front and rear)
Weight: 4,400 lbs.

HRG **1100/1500**

Other than Morgan, no company stuck so resolutely to one style of car as HRG, which produced one basic model that remained essentially unchanged for more than 20 years. The HRG is a real sports car.

"...a magical experience."

"There's no doubt the HRG appeals to the string-backed gloved, cap-wearing sports car fanatic who doesn't mind a bit of discomfort in exchange for an exciting drive. By today's standards, it's certainly not fast, but that doesn't mean it's not enjoyable—or a great sports car. It has a near-perfect set of transmission ratios and incredibly sharp quick-ratio steering box. The ride is firm, but a drive in this car is still a magical experience."

An austere cockpit transports the driver back to the vintage age of motoring.

935 The first HRG appears with its vintage-yle sports bodywork. All but e earliest cars have 1.5-liter nger-based engines.

938 An 1100 model rives with a smaller engine.

e full-width Aerodynamic as launched in 1946.

949 An HRG 1100 model wins its class at e 24 Hours of Le Mans.

class win at Le Mans was a otable achievement for HRG.

953 The 1100 model is now available nly by special order.

955 An all-new win Cam model arrives.

956 HRG ceases ar production concentrate on other ngineering work.

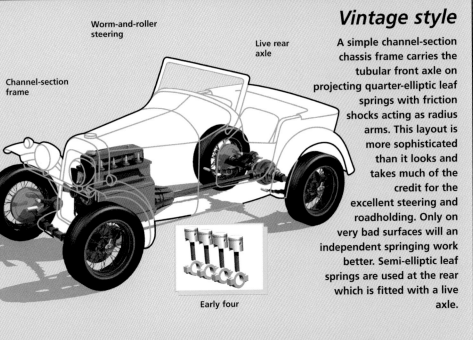

Worm-and-roller steering

Live rear axle

Channel-section frame

Early four

Vintage style

A simple channel-section chassis frame carries the tubular front axle on projecting quarter-elliptic leaf springs with friction shocks acting as radius arms. This layout is more sophisticated than it looks and takes much of the credit for the excellent steering and roadholding. Only on very bad surfaces will an independent springing work better. Semi-elliptic leaf springs are used at the rear which is fitted with a live axle.

THE POWER PACK

Modified Singer blocks

HRG was loyal to its chosen engine supplier, Singer, which was part of the Rootes group. HRGs used two sizes, an 1100 and a 1500. Each was considerably modified for use in the HRG, having twin SU carburetors, a smaller stroke and the installation of an HRG crankshaft, pistons, camshaft and larger valves to replace the original Singer parts. In 1953, the 1.5-liter engine was changed from that based on the Singer Super Twelve to the more square SM 1500 engine. HRG later developed a new top end for this engine using twin overhead camshafts in a light-alloy cylinder head.

HRG Twin Cam

Most HRGs differ from each other since they were built very much to individual customer preferences. The 1500 is a better all-round car than the smaller-engined 1100. The Twin Cam of 1955-1956 looks completely different and is very rare.

The regular HRG gave vintage driving thrills to loyal customers into the 1950s.

HRG **1100/1500**

The HRG was also a formidable performer in off-road motoring events such as trials. Along with the pre-war Frazer Nash, it is the quintessential, no-nonsense, British sports car.

Singer-derived engine

The basic engine block almost invariably came from Singer, a good choice at the time since the engines are well-suited to the sporty role. HRG performed its own head work and fitted a new crankshaft that reduced the stroke so capacity fell below the 1.5-liter limit in motorsports.

Good ground clearance

Trialing enthusiasts were grateful for the generous ground clearance offered by the HRG chassis. At six inches, this was enough to ford the sort of mud tracks found in trial events and enough to dodge protruding rocks.

Wire wheels

The HRG has classic wire wheels. Initially, these came in vintage-style measurements: 17 inches in diameter and shod with very narrow 4.75-inch tires. However, later cars have 16-inch wheels and 5.50-inch tires.

Two wheelbase lengths

Depending on engine size, the HRG chassis came in two lengths. The 1100 model uses a 99.5-inch wheelbase; the larger 1500 model measures in at 103 inches and is correspondingly longer overall.

Vintage bodystyle

In style, the bodywork is a throwback to the early 1930s. Each HRG was built by hand, using aluminum formed into various styles around the same theme. There are cutaway doors and a squared-off tail. There is even a surprising amount of luggage room behind the two bucket-type seats.

Specifications
1939 HRG 1500

ENGINE

Type: Inline four-cylinder
Construction: Cast-iron block and head
Valve gear: Two valves per cylinder operated by a single overhead camshaft
Bore and stroke: 2.68 in. x 4.06 in.
Displacement: 1,496 cc
Compression ratio: 7.0:1
Induction system: Two SU carburetors
Maximum power: 61 bhp at 4,800 rpm
Maximum torque: 77 lb-ft at 2,800 rpm
Top speed: 84 mph
0–60 mph: 18.1 sec.

TRANSMISSION

Four-speed manual

BODY/CHASSIS

Separate chassis with aluminum two-door sports body

SPECIAL FEATURES

An old-fashioned grease gun is included in the engine bay.

The HRG uses the common twin SU carburetor setup.

RUNNING GEAR

Steering: Worm-and-roller
Front suspension: Beam axle with quarter-elliptic leaf springs and shock absorbers
Rear suspension: Live axle with semi-elliptic leaf springs and shock absorbers
Brakes: Drums (front and rear)
Wheels: Wires, 17-in. dia.
Tires: 4.75 x 17

DIMENSIONS

Length: 144.0 in.   **Width:** 55.0 in.
Height: 52.0 in.   **Wheelbase:** 103.0 in.
Track: 48.0 in. (front), 45.0 in. (rear)
Weight: 1,620 lbs.

Hudson TERRAPLANE

By the mid 1930s, Terraplanes were considered to be inexpensive, rugged and reliable automobiles. But that was to ignore the fact that these cars had a number of ingenious design features that set them aside from their more mainstream rivals from Ford and Chevrolet.

"...its appeal is obvious."

"You don't drive a Terraplane to go fast. Revel instead in the comfort of the softly sprung chassis and the refinement from such an apparently crude, simple engine. The side-valve six is surprisingly quiet. Its long stroke gives a large torque output at low rpm so it will pull from incredibly slow speeds in top gear. Add light steering once the car is underway, and very effective brakes and its appeal is obvious."

The spartan cabin includes a speedometer and a unique steering column-mounted semi-automatic gear shift selector.

1924 Hudson develops a flathead, side-valve, six-cylinder engine for the new Essex Six.

1932 The first Terraplane appears. It was designed to undercut rivals from Ford and Chevrolet.

The most famous Hudson is the Hornet, made from 1949-1952.

1934 The Terraplane range is improved. The biggest news this year is the introduction of 'Axleflex'—a design that combines a beam front axle and an independent front suspension. The bodies are also restyled.

Dating from 1954, the compact Jet was the last true Hudson.

1947 The last link with the Terraplane comes to an end. The 212-cubic inch, side-valve six engine that began life in the stylish coupe was replaced with a larger 262-cubic inch engine.

UNDER THE SKIN

Channel section frame

Semi-automatic gear shift

Live rear axle

Flathead six

Spirit of the age

Like most cars of the time, the Hudson is built on a massive channel-section frame. It is a large central 'X' member that is used to give it extra reinforcement. A beam axle at the front and a live axle at the rear are mounted to the chassis. Both are sprung by semi-elliptic leaf springs and damped by telescopic shock absorbers. Naturally, brakes are drums all around, but there are advanced features like the 'Electric Hand' semi-automatic gear shifter.

THE POWER PACK

Old faithful

Hudson's flathead, six engine was already an old design by 1936 but had been steadily improved since it first appeared in 1924. It is a cast-iron unit with a three-bearing crank-shaft and sidevalves operated upward by block-mounted camshafts. One oddity, even for the time, is the lack of full-pressure lubrication to the bearings, although oiling improvements were made in 1934 when the veteran engine was stretched to 212 cubic inches. This, along with a low 6.3:1 compression ratio, was enough to give the Terraplane 88 bhp and surprising performance—0–60 mph in 23.2 seconds.

Short-lived

Although they started life under the Essex brand, the Terraplanes soon became a make in their own right. From 1936, they adopted a tasteful wraparound style grill. They were fast too, able to reach 60 mph in under 27 seconds and top 80 mph. Most desirable of all are perhaps the coupes and convertibles. A short production run means rarity today.

The Terraplane lasted only through 1937.

Hudson **TERRAPLANE**

Even though Terraplanes were not intended to be the most flamboyant and stylish cars on the road, features like the attractive grill helped make these cars stand out in a crowd.

Side-valve engine

In an L-head sidevalve engine like the 3.5-liter Hudson six, both the intake and exhaust valves are on one side of the engine. Effectively, they work upsidedown, compared with an overhead-valve engine, with the combustion chambers in the head but to one side of the engine over the valves.

Low-pressure tires

To make its cars as comfortable as possible, Hudson had a tendency to fit larger, wider tires than its rival companies. These also ran at a relatively low pressure to improve the ride.

Welded-on body

Although the Terraplane had an unusual and immensely strong steel chassis for its time, Hudson made the whole car stiffer by welding on the all-steel bodywork at more than 30 points rather than simply bolting it in place like other manufacturers were doing.

Solid front axle

Hudson's normal front-suspension system was more complicated than most. It fitted a radius arm on each side that was bolted to a solid axle. These ran back from the axle to pivots on the frame and provided better location than the semi-elliptic leaf springs could manage by them-selves. They also provide a measure of antidive under severe braking.

Reserve brake system

In case the hydraulic system failed (and these were the days before dual circuits), Hudson developed Duo-Automatic as a safety feature. Should the pedal get near the floor, it operates a cable to activate the rear brakes.

Specifications
1936 Hudson Terraplane

ENGINE
Type: Inline six cylinder
Construction: Cast-iron block and head
Valve gear: Two valves operated by single camshaft mounted on side of block
Bore and stroke: 3.0 in. x 5.0 in.
Displacement: 212 c.i.
Compression ratio: 6.0:1
Induction system: Single downdraft Carter carburetor
Maximum power: 88 bhp at 3,800 rpm
Maximum torque: Not quoted
Top speed: 80 mph
0–60 mph: 23.2 sec.

TRANSMISSION
Three-speed manual

BODY/CHASSIS
Separate channel-section frame with X-brace and welded-on steel body

SPECIAL FEATURES

The Hudson Terraplane was known for its ornate details such as this interesting grill ornament.

A fold-out rear rumble seat can easily accommodate two people in total comfort.

RUNNING GEAR
Steering: Worm-and-sector
Front suspension: Solid axle with radius rods, semi-elliptic leaf springs and telescopic shock absorbers
Rear suspension: Live axle with semi-elliptic leaf springs and telescopic shock absorbers
Brakes: Drums (front and rear)
Wheels: Pressed steel, 16-in. dia.
Tires: 6.00 x 16

DIMENSIONS
Length: 195.0 in. **Width:** 70.0 in.
Height: 70.8 in. **Wheelbase:** 115.0 in.
Track: 56.0 in. (front), 57.5 in. (rear)
Weight: 2,740 lbs.

Invicta **S-TYPE**

While it wasn't as famous as the 4¹/₂ Litre Bentley, the low-chassis Invicta S-type nevertheless had both the performance and the reliability of a Bentley and was a competitive racer as well as a Monte Carlo Rally winner.

"...incredibly strong engine."

"Because it has a very hard ride, the Invicta is not the most comfortable car. This, however, allows it to corner at remarkably high speeds for the 1930s. It has a tendency to break away without warning because it lacks grip from the relatively thin tires and thus requires skilful driving. Its best feature is the incredibly strong, smooth engine which accelerates all the way to 100 mph. This is backed up by what are, for the era, very powerful brakes."

The layout of the Invicta's cabin is dominated by the large steering wheel.

Milestones

1924 Captain A.N.C. Mackling founds Invicta cars in Surrey. Early models use 3 liter, Meadows, in-line six engines.

Donald Healey drove an S-type to victory in the grueling 1931 Monte Carlo Rally.

1928 A larger Meadows engine leads to the creation of the 4½ liter NLC.

1929 Although sales suffer during the Great Depression the Sports or S type is launched. It features a new, underslung chassis.

Only 76 S-types were built.

1931 Donald Healey uses an Invicta S-type to win the Monte Carlo Rally. He also comes in second in 1932.

1934 It's the end of the road for Invicta. Sales are too slow and Mackling soon leaves to form the Railton Co. In all, 76 S-Types are made, of which 56 still survive.

UNDER THE SKIN

Cockpit-adjustable friction dampers

Semi-elliptic leaf-spring rear suspension

Meadows four-speed transmission

In-line six

Flexing chassis

The Invicta used an immensely strong chassis with deep siderails but with very little crossbracing for the Meadows four-speed transmission. Thus, that chassis flex was quite noticeable. The S-type is lower than the standard model because the chassis rails run under the rear axle. Like the front axle, the rear is located and sprung by semi-elliptic leaf springs and friction dampers that can be adjustable from the cockpit.

THE POWER PACK

Meadows engine

Invicta bought in its major components and used Meadows, in-line, six-cylinder engines to power all of its early cars. By the 1930s, the engine had been stretched to 4.5 liters with a larger bore, but it was still a very undersquare, long-stroke design, which gave it its characteristic huge torque output and flexible, effortless top gear performance. Both the crankcase and cylinder head are alloy, and the two overhead valves per cylinder are opened with pushrods. Two spark plugs per cylinder are used, each with its own ignition system. This enables the engine to produce 115 bhp at 3,200 rpm.

Peak performer

The most famous S-type is the one used by racing driver Raymond Mays. Considerably lighter than the standard car, the engine was tuned to give 160 bhp at 3,900 rpm. It made the Invicta an almost unbeatable hillclimb car and extremely fast around England's famous banked Brooklands track.

The fast S-Type made an excellent competition car in the 1930s.

Invicta S-TYPE

Invicta showed what could be done with outsourced components. Separate manufacturers supplied the mechanics and the bodywork but everything came together to make a 1930s supercar with lots of character.

Coachbuilt bodies

Different bodies could be specified for the 4½ Litre's chassis, but the S-type typically had long, low bodywork built either by Vanden Plas or Carbodies Coachbuilders.

Six-cylinder engine

The Meadows company supplied engines to a number of car makers. Tuning was easy because of its advanced, crossflow design with exhaust and intake manifolds on different sides of the engine.

Four-speed transmission

With so much torque the engine can use top gear at virtually any speed. But to get the best from the transmission, double clutching is necessary.

Flexible exhaust pipes

The flexible exhaust pipes are very stylish. They are connected to the exhaust manifold and project out of one side of the long hood. The hood is hinged in the center and can be opened from either side.

Underslung chassis

The standard Invicta 4½ is a tall, upright model, but the S-type is much more low slung and streamlined. This is achieved by designing the chassis rails to curve under the rear axle. This arrangement requires very stiff springs and limited wheel travel to stop the axle from hitting the chassis.

Specifications
1930 Invicta S-Type

ENGINE

Type: Meadows in-line six cylinder

Construction: Alloy block and head

Valve gear: Two valves per cylinder operated by a single block-mounted camshaft via pushrods and rockers

Bore and stroke: 3.48 in. x 4.75 in.

Displacement: 4,467 cc

Compression ratio: 8:1

Induction system: Twin SU carburetors

Maximum power: 115 bhp at 3,200 rpm

Maximum torque: Not quoted

Top speed: 100 mph

0–60 mph: 14.4 sec.

TRANSMISSION

Meadows four-speed manual

BODY/CHASSIS

Steel ladder-frame chassis with separate open coachbuilt body

SPECIAL FEATURES

The side mounted handbrake is easily accessible. It is located outside the car, right next to the spare tire.

Protective covers over the side-mounted exhaust pipes prevent burns on over-curious passengers.

RUNNING GEAR

Steering: Marles worm-and-roller

Front suspension: Beam axle with semi-elliptic leaf springs and adjustable shocks

Rear suspension: Live axle with semi-elliptic leaf springs and adjustable friction shock absorbers

Brakes: Mechanically operated finned drums (front and rear)

Wheels: Wire spoke

Tires: Dunlop 19.0 x 6.00 in.

DIMENSIONS

Length: 156.0 in. **Width:** 60.0 in.

Height: 52.0 in. **Wheelbase:** 118.0 in.

Track: 52.0 in. (front and rear)

Weight: 3,248 lbs.

Itala GRAND PRIX

During the early 1900s huge-engined racers ruled the Grand Prix circuit. With a muscular 14.8-liter engine, the Itala could achieve speeds over 100 mph ensuring great success in major international Grand Prix events.

"...perfect weight distribution."

"In the hands of a skilled driver, the Itala can achieve top speeds of more than 100 mph. Despite narrow tires and strongly cambered springs, the car's handling is a delight, and you can take advantage of the lack of grip to induce four-wheel drifts when exiting turns. Its steering is surprisingly light and the ride is rather comfortable. Gearshifts can be made smoothly and quite easily, without the need to double clutch the transmission."

Among the Itala's brass fittings, only the speedo is a recognizable feature.

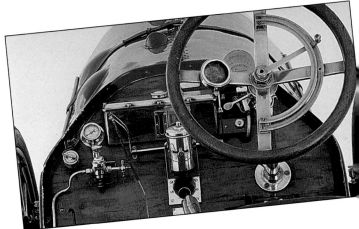

Milestones

1905 Alberto Balocco is appointed as chief engineer to begin work on the first series of giant racing cars designed to bring the young company instant publicity. Later that year, a 100-bhp Itala wins the 311-mile Coppa Florio at Brescia.

Five Italas entered the 1907 Targa Florio in Sicily, finishing 1-2-4-5.

1906 Fitted with twin fuel tanks, a 7,433-cc Itala finishes first in the longest ever endurance race—the Peking-Paris event.

In 1989, Fiat ran the newly restored Itala from Peking to Paris—a total of 8,000 miles.

1907 A new single formula is applied to all major racing events. Parameters include a maximum bore size of 6.10 inches for four-cylinder engines. Subsequently, the Itala Grand Prix emerges with a huge 14.8-liter engine.

UNDER THE SKIN

No front brakes

Rear-wheel drive

Engine mounted behind front axle

Huge inline four

Conventional chassis

The chassis used on the Itala Grand Prix is a conventional ladder-type frame, stiffened at the front by the rigidly mounted engine. The front suspension is non-independent, an H-section forged beam sprung by semi-elliptic leaf springs. The live rear axle relies on semi-elliptic leaf springs but without friction shocks. Power is transmitted through a 64-plate clutch to a four-speed trans-mission mounted at the midpoint of the chassis.

THE POWER PACK

Cast-iron cylinders

The Itala's huge 14.8-liter engine is made up of four iron cylinders cast in pairs and is mounted behind the front axle line to improve weight distribution. A single camshaft in the crankcase operates both the side exhaust and the over-head intake valves by pushrods and rockers. The camshaft also drives two vertical shafts passing between each pair of cylinders. Ignition timing can be advanced and retarded by moving a lever back and forth. An updraft carburetor with a two-branch manifold fuels the huge cylinders to give 11 mpg. Like most cars of this era, the Itala's transmission is mounted directly behind the massive, four-cylinder engine.

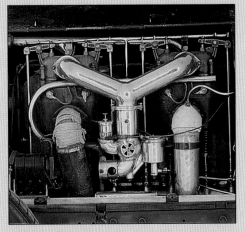

Overhauled

Fiat totally overhauled the famous Peking-Paris Itala of 1907 and set out to repeat the epic journey in 1989. The 7.4-liter Itala covered the whole distance without any mechanical problems. New beaded-edge tires were specially made by Pirelli on original tire machines.

Rough race tracks demanded that cars carried a number of spare tires.

121

Itala GRAND PRIX

French Grand Prix racing regulations were the most relaxed of all, with no limit placed on engine size, but fuel consumption was limited to 10 mpg. Consequently, the Itala appeared with a huge engine and achieved 11 mpg.

Iron cylinders

The Itala's engine is made of two huge pairs of cast-iron cylinders cast together. These are mounted onto a light aluminum-alloy crankcase.

Intake-over-exhaust design

The intake valves are mounted overhead, while the exhaust valves are side-mounted.

Separate transmission

Unlike modern cars that have their transmissions mounted directly onto the engine, the Itala's transmission is positioned behind the engine.

Advance/retard mechanism

Ignition timing can be varied by an advance/retard mechanism mounted on the steering wheel instead of being fitted on the distributor.

Fuel pressure pump

Fuel is fed to the carburetor by a rear-mounted fuel tank and is pressurized by an externally mounted hand pump.

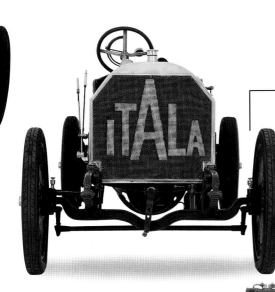

No front brakes

In common with nearly all road and racing cars, front brakes were virtually unheard of before World War I. The only advantage to this was a reduction in front unsprung weight.

Wooden spokes

In the early days of motoring, manufacturers used wooden-spoke wheels. They are known as 'artillery' wheels, as they were used on gun carriages.

Single carburetor

A single updraft carburetor fuels all four huge cylinders with a Y-shaped manifold. Each branchfeeds a pair of cylinders.

Specifications
1907 Itala Grand Prix

ENGINE

Type: Inline four-cylinder

Construction: Four cylinders (cast in pairs) with aluminum-alloy crankcase

Valve gear: Two valves per cylinder operated by a block-mounted camshaft via pushrods and rockers

Bore and stroke: 6.22 in. x 6.30 in.

Displacement: 14,759 cc

Compression ratio: 4.5:1

Induction system: Single Itala updraft carburetor

Maximum power: 120 bhp at 1,600 rpm

Maximum torque: Not quoted

Top speed: 106 mph

0–60 mph: 16.0 sec.

TRANSMISSION

Separate four-speed manual

BODY/CHASSIS

Steel ladder frame with open racing two-seater body

SPECIAL FEATURES

A transmission brake makes up for the Itala's single rear brake.

The four-speed transmission is operated by an outboard-mounted shift lever.

RUNNING GEAR

Steering: Worm-and-wheel

Front suspension: H-section beam axle, semi-elliptic leaf springs and friction shock absorbers

Rear suspension: Live axle with semi-elliptic leaf springs

Brakes: Internal expanding drums (rear only)

Wheels: Wooden-spoke artillery type

Tires: Beaded-edge, 36 x 4.13 in. (front), 35.2 x 5.3 in. (rear)

DIMENSIONS

Length: 165.0 in.   **Width:** 68.1 in.

Height: 53.5 in.   **Wheelbase:** 126.0 in.

Track: 60.0 in. (front and rear)

Weight: 3,142 lbs.

UK 1934–1937

Lagonda RAPIER

Lagonda earned a reputation for building large, rugged and powerful cars. Naturally, it was a surprise when this British automobile company introduced the scaled-down Rapier, a beautifully designed and exceptionally well built machine.

"...a very deceiving look."

"Rapiers have a very deceiving look. Test drivers were amazed at the car's outstanding performance in every area. The tiny twin-cam revs higher than most cars of the period. Its chassis gives outstanding handling and road holding. It takes corners more safely and at much greater speeds than any of its rivals. Although the ride is stiff eliminating any cornering roll, it isn't unbearably harsh. The high-geared steering is very responsive."

Well trimmed, yet tastefully restrained, the Rapier's cockpit is an inviting place.

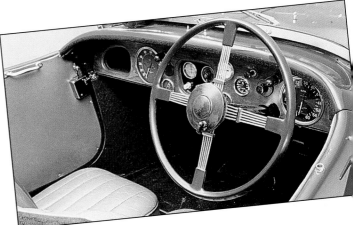

1933 Lagonda introduces the Rapier at the Olympia Show in London. The response is so good that Lagonda orders 500 engines.

This lightweight Rapier racer is powered by a 1,086 cc engine.

1934 Before it enters production, Lagonda lengthens the wheelbase to 100 inches. A short version finishes 13th at Le Mans.

The largest of the mid 1930 Lagondas is the 4½-liter LG45.

1935 After suffering enormous financial problems, Lagonda goes into receivership. A new company, Rapier Cars Ltd, is formed.

1943 Rapier Cars finally goes out of business. The last cars are sold in 1937. Between Lagonda and Rapier Cars, approximately 500 automobiles were built.

UNDER THE SKIN

Ladder-type chassis

Leaf-sprung suspension front and rear

Girling four-wheel drum brakes

High-revving four

Big framed

For a small car, the Rapier has a massive chassis with two main flanged side rails kicking up at the rear to clear the axle and rising up at the front to carry the engine. Six tubular cross-members give the car its stiff composure. It has a beam front axle and live rear axle, both on semi-elliptic leaf springs with friction shocks. The brakes are large, rod-operated Girling drums, and steering is by cam-and-roller.

THE POWER PACK

Hi-tech wonder

The tiny 1.1-liter, twin-cam was originally designed to be an all-alloy engine with cast-iron dry liners, but to keep costs down, it was made from cast-iron instead. This added greater weight to the car, but also made the engine immensely strong. A fully counter-balanced crankshaft on three bearings, very strong connecting rods and efficient hemispherical combustion chambers enable a sustained high engine speed. The angled valves are opened by two chain-driven, overhead camshafts. With this engine, the little Rapier could sprint to 60 mph just under 22 seconds and reach almost 80 mph flat out.

Blown away

After the Rapier design was sold to Rapier Cars, a small number of supercharged versions were built that could really exploit the strength of the twin-cam engine. These cars were able to reach 50 mph in under 10 seconds and had an impressive top speed close to 90 mph.

Adding a supercharger turned the Rapier into a real performer.

Lagonda RAPIER

The appearance of the Rapier depended on which one of the four outside coachbuilders actually designed and built the body. Most common was the classic two-seater 1930s sports car, but there were also four-seaters.

Twin-cam engine

The Rapier's extremely strong and high-revving four-cylinder twin-cam was superb. There was great scope for tuning an already powerful engine, but power outputs were never revealed.

Alloy oil pan

The engine is all cast-iron, except for the oil pan which is made from finned alloy. It holds a more than adequate amount of o for such a small engin

Wire wheels

Almost all 1930s sports cars had light and strong wire-spoke wheels. All that is needed for wheel changes is a mallet to knock the center spinner on and off.

Four-wheel handbrake

Lagonda took the requirement for a handbrake very seriously. Where other manufacturers had it operating on just the rear wheels, Lagonda connected it to all four so there was actually a chance of it providing some useful stopping power.

Advance/retard system

The Rapier has a very prehistoric engine management system. The engine is kept in time by the help of an advance/retard lever on the steering column. The timing is retarded to start and then advanced as the temperatures rise and speeds increase.

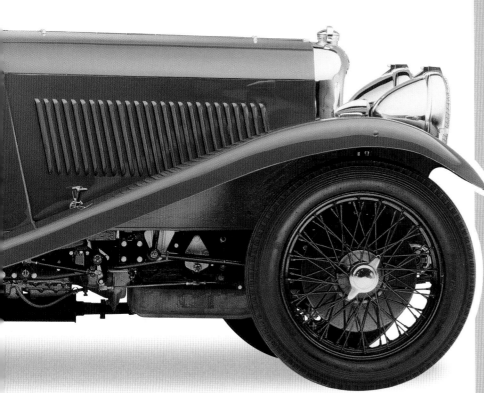

Specifications
1934 Lagonda Rapier

ENGINE

Type: In-line four-cylinder

Construction: Cast-iron block and head

Valve gear: Two valves per cylinder operated by twin chain-driven overhead camshafts

Bore and stroke: 2.46 in. x 3.54 in.

Displacement: 1,104 cc

Compression ratio: N/A

Induction system: Two SU carburetors

Maximum power: Not quoted

Maximum torque: Not quoted

Top speed: 78 mph

0–60 mph: 21.8 sec.

TRANSMISSION

ENV pre-selector four-speed

BODY/CHASSIS

Separate steel ladder frame chassis with tubular crossmembers and customer choice of bodywork

SPECIAL FEATURES

Like most cars of the period, the Rapier has an externally mounted starter crank handle.

The Rapier followed the fashion of its time by using free-standing headlights.

RUNNING GEAR

Steering: Cam-and-roller

Front suspension: Solid axle with semi-elliptic leaf springs and Hartford friction shock absorbers

Rear suspension: Beam axle with semi-elliptic leaf springs and parallel Hartford friction shock absorbers

Brakes: Girling drums, 13-in. dia. (front and rear)

Wheels: Knock-on/off wire-spoke, 19-in. dia.

Tires: 4.50 x 19

DIMENSIONS

Length: 154.0 in.   **Width:** 60.0 in.

Height: 54.0 in.   **Wheelbase:** 100.0 in.

Track: 45.8 in. (front), 48.0 in. (rear)

Weight: 1,904 lbs.

 **ITALY** 1922–1931

Lancia **LAMBDA**

A true milestone car, the Lambda has a compact V4 engine, independent front suspension and revolutionary monocoque frameless construction. Not surprisingly, the Lambda was an outstanding performer.

"...beautiful balance and poise."

"In such a light car the smooth and lively 2.1-liter V4 engine offers more than enough power and can cruise happily all day long at a brisk 50 mph. Even better is the Lambda's handling, with decisive steering. Because the Lambda has beautiful balance and poise, it can be driven surprisingly quickly on twisty roads without suffering from a harsh ride. Comfort is as good as can be expected from a 1920s car, but it always feels alert and powerful."

Back to the golden age: The Lambda has typical period charm with its sparse cabin.

1922 The original Lambda is launched at the Geneva Motor show. Initially, only one 'Torpedo' body style available.

The luxury DiLambda was powered by a 4.0-liter V8.

1924 A third series is announced. The fourth series car of the same year has an improved engine.

1925 The fifth series receives a four-speed transmission.

The later Lancia Artena used a 2.0-liter V4.

1926 A larger 59-bhp, 2,370-cc engine introduced for the seventh series car.

1928 The eighth series Lambda has a large capacity 2,570-cc engine.

1931 The ninth series has an improved electrical system, but the Lambda replaced by the DiLambda.

UNDER THE SKIN

Leaf-sprung rear axle

Skeletal steel frame

Four-wheel drum brakes

Unit body/frame

It was a boat trip, so the story goes, that got Vincenzo Lancia thinking about the one-piece hull of a ship and how it was more structurally sound than that of the typical car of the period. The Lambda uses a skeletal steel construction with cut-outs for the doors. The steel 'Torpedo'-style open-topped bodywork was riveted to the chassis.

Lightweight V4

THE POWER PACK

High-tech wonder

The V-configuration engine wasn't an entirely new concept to Lancia, as patents for a V8 had existed since 1915. The 'V' of the Lambda Tipo 67 engine was very narrow at 13 degrees and featured a shaft-driven overhead camshaft and an aluminum cylinder block for lightness and strength. The short, sturdy crankshaft ran in three main bearings, while the cylinder head was cast in iron. The original transmission was a three-speed unit with a multi-plate dry clutch and a short-throw shifter.

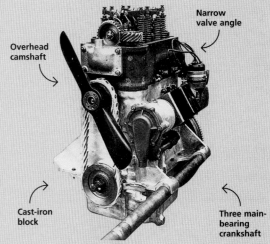

Overhead camshaft

Narrow valve angle

Cast-iron block

Three main-bearing crankshaft

Pinnacle

Vincenzo Lancia founded his company in 1906, and for many years Lancias were renowned for their advanced engineering and quality construction. Out of all the Lambdas, the final ninth series, with the larger V4 and improved electrics, is the best.

The Lancia Lambda offered many technical advancements for its day.

Lancia **LAMBDA**

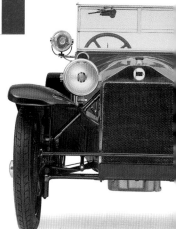

The Lambda was a technical marvel and made the reputation of the Turin company with beautifully engineered drivers' cars. It rates as one of the most significant cars of the century.

V4 engine

Extremely potent for its size, the Lambda's narrow-angle V4 has an overhead camshaft and an aluminum block for strength and lightness. It grew in size from 2,120 cc to 2,570 cc by the end of the 1920s.

Four-wheel brakes

Brakes on the front wheels were by no means universal in 1922, but the Lambda had a powerful system using 12-inch four-wheel drums, operated by steel wire cables.

Three- and four-speed transmissions

Up to the fifth series, all Lambdas were three-speeders with a multi-plate dry clutch and a two-piece driveshaft with Hardy Spicer couplings. However, from this series onward all models benefited from a four-speed unit, improving both gear shifts and performance.

Rear suspension

At the back, the Lambda has a live axle and semi-elliptic leaf springs. It was Vincenzo Lancia's original intention to build the car without a differential because of its expected lightness, but his engineers persuaded him not to do this.

Monocoque construction

The Lambda's strength comes from its its one-piece skeletal structure made from thick pressed sheet metal. It is extremely rigid compared with the contemporary separate chassis construction cars.

Independent front suspension

The sliding-pillar system was used by Lancia because of its comfort. Only a handful of other cars had independent front suspension at the time.

Specifications
1922 Lancia Lambda

ENGINE

Type: V4

Construction: Light-alloy block and cast-iron cylinder heads

Valve gear: Gear-driven overhead camshaft with vertical valve springs

Bore and stroke: 2.95 in. x 4.72 in.

Displacement: 2,120 cc

Compression ratio: 5.0:1

Induction system: Zenith 36 HK carburetor

Maximum power: 49 bhp at 3,250 rpm

Maximum torque: Not quoted

Top speed: 74 mph

10-30 mph: 14.0 sec.

TRANSMISSION

Three-speed manual

BODY/CHASSIS

Monocoque construction with open Torpedo bodywork

SPECIAL FEATURES

Large toolboxes are built into the Lambda's running boards.

A large, externally mounted horn was necessary in the 1920s.

RUNNING GEAR

Steering: Worm-and-wheel

Front suspension: Sliding pillar

Rear suspension: Live axle with leaf springs

Brakes: Mechanically-operated drums, 12-in. dia. (front and rear)

Wheels: Rudge Whitworth wires

Tires: 5.7 in. x 17 in.

DIMENSIONS

Length: 195.8 in.   **Width:** 65.7 in.

Height: Not quoted

Wheelbase: 122.1 in.

Track: 55.1 in. (front), 56.4 in. (rear)

Weight: 2,700 lbs.

Lincoln **ZEPHYR**

Introduced as a 'junior' Lincoln, the Zephyr was the car that saved the division during the late 1930s. It revitalized the range and brought a combination of style and V12 power at a price rivals could not match.

"...relaxed performance."

"Effortless, relaxed performance sums up the Zephyr. The V12 is silky-smooth and pulls from extremely low revs yet still has enough top-end power to move the car to a relaxed 87 mph. With its synchromesh gears and a light clutch, gear shifts are easy. The steering is light thanks to the low-geared ratio, with 4.5 turns lock to lock. Despite having a fairly dated suspension, the ride is smooth, making long-distance journeys an enjoyable experience."

A distinctive feature of the Zephyr is its large-faced, center-mounted speedometer.

934 Briggs exhibits a concept car designed by John Tjaarda at the Chicago World's Fair. It has a rear-mounted V8 engine, fully independent suspension, unitary construction and radically new streamlined body styling.

e Zephyr was initially offered in two- and four-door sedan forms.

936 A production Zephyr goes on sale. It is powered by a 267-cubic inch V12 and is styled is by Bob Gregorie.

938 Zephyrs get longer wheelbase and styling changes including mouth organ grill.

restyle for 1938 set a styling trend for the rest of the decade.

940 The Zephyr gains an all-new body and a V12 stroked to 292 cubic inches. The convertible sedan is dropped, but production reaches 21,944.

942 Civilian auto production is suspended.

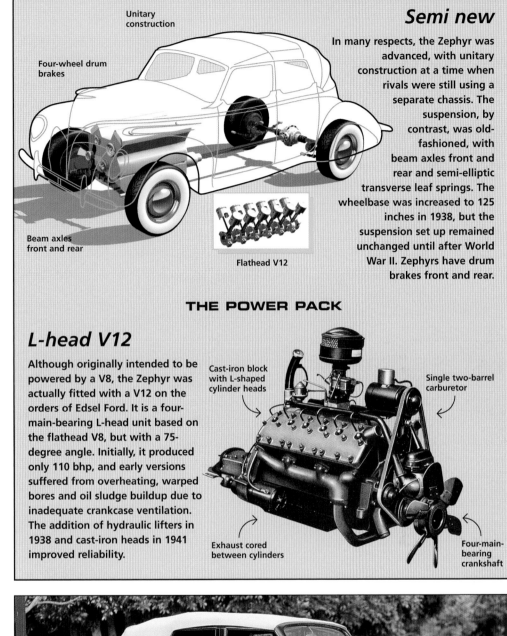

Labels in diagram:
Unitary construction
Four-wheel drum brakes
Beam axles front and rear
Flathead V12

Semi new

In many respects, the Zephyr was advanced, with unitary construction at a time when rivals were still using a separate chassis. The suspension, by contrast, was old-fashioned, with beam axles front and rear and semi-elliptic transverse leaf springs. The wheelbase was increased to 125 inches in 1938, but the suspension set up remained unchanged until after World War II. Zephyrs have drum brakes front and rear.

THE POWER PACK

L-head V12

Although originally intended to be powered by a V8, the Zephyr was actually fitted with a V12 on the orders of Edsel Ford. It is a four-main-bearing L-head unit based on the flathead V8, but with a 75-degree angle. Initially, it produced only 110 bhp, and early versions suffered from overheating, warped bores and oil sludge buildup due to inadequate crankcase ventilation. The addition of hydraulic lifters in 1938 and cast-iron heads in 1941 improved reliability.

Engine labels:
Cast-iron block with L-shaped cylinder heads
Single two-barrel carburetor
Exhaust cored between cylinders
Four-main-bearing crankshaft

Open air

For its day, the Zephyr was revolutionary in many ways, with its unitary construction and trend-setting styling. Perhaps the most desirable of all body styles is the four-door convertible, built only in small numbers and lasting through 1939.

Convertible Zephyr sedans were offered only in 1938 and 1939.

Lincoln ZEPHYR

The Zephyr was a curious mixture of new technology—with unitary construction and smooth styling—combined with the old, including mechanical drum brakes and beam axle suspension front and rear.

V12 engine

The Zephyr V12 is a compromise as it is based on the flathead V8. Quiet and refined, it is tuned for torque, not horsepower. The biggest problem is reliability and, consequently, many owners chose to replace the V12 with later Mercury flathead V8s.

Beam axles

Due to the stubbornness of Henry Ford, the Zephyr retained beam-axle suspensi... with transverse leaf springs. To improve the handling, adjustable hydrauli... shocks were offered

Three-speed transmission

Geared more for torque than power, the V12 is perfectly mated to the three-speed manual transmission. Synchromesh is fitted to second and top gear to make shifting easier.

Unitary construction

Adopting aircraft techniques, the Zephyr has a light, steel-covered girder-like framework onto which the body is welded. This results in a lighter structure than most rival luxury cars of the time.

Vacuum wipers

There is no electric motor for the windshield wipers, so they are powered by the inlet manifold vacuum. The speed of the wipers varies with engine load, resulting in a slower wiper speed up hills.

Steel disc wheels

By 1936, most American automobile manufacturers had abandoned wire wheels in favor of discs, and the Zephyr was no exception.

Two-speed axle

From 1936 to 1940 a two-speed Columbia rear axle was offered. This effectively doubles the number of gears, giving six forward speeds.

Specifications

1939 Lincoln Zephyr

ENGINE

Type: V12

Construction: Cast-iron block and alloy heads

Valve gear: Two sidevalves per cylinder operated by a side-mounted camshaft

Bore and stroke: 2.75 in. x 3.75 in.

Displacement: 267 c.i.

Compression ratio: 7.2:1

Induction system: Single two-barrel downdraft carburetor

Maximum power: 110 bhp at 3,900 rpm

Maximum torque: 180 lb-ft at 3,500 rpm

Top speed: 87 mph

0–60 mph: 16.0 sec.

TRANSMISSION

Three-speed manual

BODY/CHASSIS

Unitary steel construction with four-door convertible sedan body.

SPECIAL FEATURES

A special V12 engine was commissioned for the Zephyr.

The spare tire mount can be hinged outward for easier luggage access.

RUNNING GEAR

Steering: Worm-and-roller

Front suspension: Beam axle with transverse semi-elliptic leaf spring and hydraulic shock absorbers

Rear suspension: Live axle with transverse semi-elliptic leaf spring and hydraulic shock absorbers

Brakes: Drums (front and rear)

Wheels: Steel discs, 16-in. dia.

Tires: 7.00 x 16 in.

DIMENSIONS

Length: 210.0 in.   **Width:** 73.0 in.

Height: 67.0 in.   **Wheelbase:** 122.0 in.

Track: 55.5 in. (front), 58.25 in. (rear)

Weight: 3,790 lbs.

Mercedes 540K

A superb supercharged straight-eight engine made the Mercedes 500, and the subsequent 540K, two of the greatest pre-war supercars. They were powerful, fast and had immense presence and prestige.

"...dual personality."

"The 540K has a dual personality. Without the supercharger engaged there is only 115 bhp available. But in a Special Roadster with your foot down and the supercharger blowing hard the car is an entirely different proposition. The rear swing axles contribute to high levels of cornering as long as the car is not travelling too fast. Its ride is absolutely superb thanks to the all-independent suspension and the car's great weight."

Beautiful, flowing lines of the Special Roadster are matched by an elegant yet functional interior.

Milestones

*…he unique streamlined
…utobahn Kurier looked
…credibly modern in the
…arly 1930s.*

UNDER THE SKIN

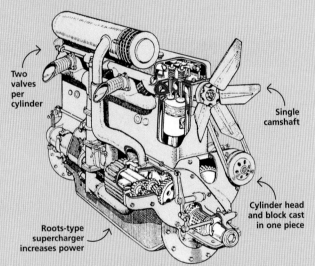

Swing-axle rear suspension

Semi-automatic
gearshifter

Sturdy ladder
chassis

Double wishbone
front suspension

Huge straight-eight

Truck-like

Because the big Mercedes
models are often required to
carry extremely heavy
bodywork the chassis is
built very sturdy. It
uses a ladder frame
with huge box
section side members.
Although the rear features
relatively simple swing axles
the front suspension uses
double wishbones. Another
advanced feature is the semi-
automatic transmission.

THE POWER PACK

Supercharged

Curiously there is nothing
advanced about the 500 or the
540K engine. It is an iron
monobloc design (i.e. head and
block cast in one piece) with a
single block-mounted camshaft
operating just two in-line valves
via pushrods and rockers. It is the
supercharger which transforms
the long-stroke (3.46 inches x
4.37 inches), 5.4-liter engine,
adding some 65 bhp for the brief
periods when it is engaged. It is
only engaged when the
accelerator pedal is pushed all
the way to the floor.

Two
valves
per
cylinder

Single
camshaft

Roots-type
supercharger
increases power

Cylinder head
and block cast
in one piece

Flamboyant

The Special Roadsters are the cream of the 540K line. Their flamboyant
flowing bodywork, designed in-house at Mercedes, suggests speed.
Without the weight of some of the other bodies they are fast cars and
nearly capable of reaching 110 mph.

*As well as stunning
looks, the Special
Roadster body also offers
reduced weight.*

Mercedes 540K

The 500 and 540K Mercedes were built in a large range of styles with the beautiful Special Roadsters some of the rarest. More conservative designs like this 1943 500K Cabrio were more common.

Independent front suspension

The Mercedes looked old-fashioned enough to have a solid front axle but in fact it features a new and effective double wishbone and coil spring independent front suspension.

Straight-eight engine

The Mercedes in-line, eight-cylinder engine was a very simple design: cast-iron with two valves per cylinder where rivals such as Bentley had four-valve-per-cylinder designs.

Clutchless gearshifter

If the driver did not wish to use the clutch he could shift from third to fourth by moving the shifter to the right and then up, parallel to third and releasing the throttle pedal.

Separate chassis

The Mercedes chassis looks as though it belongs to a truck. It is massive, with deep box section side members. The advantage of a separate chassis is that it allowed a huge range of coachbuilt bodies to be built on it.

Servo-assisted brakes

One feature where the big Mercedes is advanced is in having servo assistance for its hydraulically-operated drum brakes.

Sprung steel bumpers

Strong sprung steel bumpers were designed to absorb an impact and then spring back into shape.

Dual exhaust

To further exploit power, dual exhaust pipes are used, each carrying the exhaust gases from four of the eight cylinders.

Electric windshield wipers

he motors are installed on to the windshield instead of being mounted under the hood.

Specifications
1938 Mercedes-Benz 540K

ENGINE

Type: In-line eight cylinder
Construction: Monobloc with cast-iron head and block in unit
Valve gear: Two parallel valves per cylinder operated by single block-mounted camshaft, pushrods and rockers
Bore and stroke: 3.46 in. x 4.37 in.
Displacement: 5,401 cc
Compression ratio: 6.13:1
Induction system: Single Mercedes updraft carburetor with Roots-type supercharger
Maximum power: 115 bhp normally aspirated, 180 bhp at 3,500 rpm with supercharger engaged
Maximum torque: Not quoted
Top speed: 105 mph
0–60 mph: 17.0 sec.

TRANSMISSION

Four-speed manual with semi-automatic change on top two gears

BODY/CHASSIS

Separate ladder frame chassis with variety of bodies

SPECIAL FEATURES

Mounted on the side of the windshield is an adjustable light for reading road signs.

The crankshaft-driven supercharger is activated by a clutch.

RUNNING GEAR

Steering: Worm-and-nut
Front suspension: Double wishbones with coil springs and hydraulic shocks
Rear suspension: Swing axles with trailing arms, hydraulic shocks and twin coil springs per side
Brakes: Lockheed hydraulic drums all round
Wheels: Wire spoke, 17-in. dia.
Tires: Dunlop crossply, 7 x 17 in.

DIMENSIONS

Length: 207 in.   **Width:** 75 in.
Height: 62.5 in.   **Wheelbase:** 129.5 in.
Track: 59.5 in. (front), 58.8 in. (rear)
Weight: 5,516 lbs.

MG **18/80**

The first MG to be more than a mildly modified Morris, the 18/80 still borrowed parts such as the 2.5-liter overhead-cam straight six, but combined them to make a faster and better-handling sports car.

"...a civilized tourer."

"The 18/80 comes across as a very civilized tourer; quiet and refined, with suspension compliant enough to give a comfortable ride, unless the adjustable friction dampers are set hard to help cornering. Steering is light and direct, the gearbox and clutch easy to use and— with the Dewandre servo fitted—the brakes feel very powerful for the era. Too much weight hampers outright acceleration, but once it reaches 70 mph it can cruise there with ease."

MG fascias have always been more elaborate and sporty than standard Morris ones.

1923 Cecil Kimber
of Morris Garages, Oxford, founds MG. They specialize in putting more sporty bodies on ordinary Morris cars.

The road-racing derivative was the 18/100 or 'Tigress.'

1928 MG creates
the 18/80 from the Morris Six. It retains the overhead-cam engine.

The Midget succeeded the 18/80 as MG's primary competition car.

1929 The MKII
appears a year after the first model with some significant improvements. It has a stiffer chassis, bigger brake drums and a four- rather than a three-speed transmission. The original model is still kept in production.

1931 Production of
the MKI ends after 500 have been made.

1933 The last MKII
is built, of 236 examples.

UNDER THE SKIN

Front and rear drum brakes

Live rear axle

Front beam axle

Inline six

Morris parts

The 18/80 was MG's first car, so it made sense to use as many Morris parts as possible. They did however, improve the basic chassis frame of the Morris Six, and the bodywork was built by an outside company. Other components, like the front beam axle and live rear axle, along with their semi-elliptic leaf springs, are used unaltered. Its three-speed transmission comes from the Morris Six as well. The first cars have 12-inch drum brakes.

THE POWER PACK

Advanced design

The 18/80's engine could also be found in the ordinary Morris Six, where it must have seemed a very advanced design. Block and head are cast-iron as usual, but the valves are operated by an overhead camshaft. The two valves per cylinder are inline across the head, but although the head looks like a non-crossflow type (with carburetors and the exhaust manifold on the same side of the head), fuel goes through a tunnel across the engine to an intake manifold on the other side. The spark plugs are mounted horizontally on the intake side of the combustion chamber. Power output is 60 bhp.

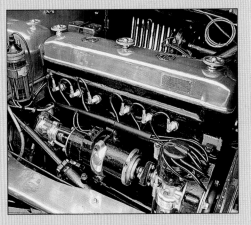

MKII

Although almost visually identical, the MKII version of the 18/80 is much improved over the original model. Top speed is unaltered, but there is much more refinement for the driver and passenger. Rarest of all are the racing 18/100 models, of which only five were made.

The MkII 18/80 is an elegant tourer with quintessential British appeal.

MG 18/80 🇬🇧

MG's 18/80 came with a wide choice of bodywork, from closed sedans and coupes to two- or four-seater convertibles. The style was that bit more adventurous to tempt buyers away from mainstream manufacturers.

Overhead-cam engine

Although the MG's 2.5-liter straight six was an overhead-cam design, the engine was not designed to rev at great speeds as its long stroke (69 mm x 110 mm) indicates. At this time, piston speeds were a limiting factor in how fast an engine could run.

Beam front ax

MG took the front axle a suspension from t contemporary Morris S which consisted of a so beam axle riding on lo semi-elliptic leaf spring The MKI had a 48-in track front and rear, b that grew to 52 inches f the MkII, which also ha wider leaf spring

Wire wheels

Tall Rudge-Whitworth wire spoke wheels were fitted because they were light and strong and had the quick release knock-on/off center spline fixing.

Wooden-frame body

MG gave the job of building the bodies for its cars to an outside company, Carbodies, in nearby Coventry. They were made in the traditional manner, with alloy panels over a wooden ash frame, with steel used for the parts that needed to be stronger, such as the fenders.

The 18/80 name

The 18/80 in the car's name referred first to the theoretical taxable horsepower, calculated to a bizarre and technically meaningless formula, and second to the real power output. In fact, little more than 60 bhp was extracted from the engine in standard form; it's just that 18/80 sounded far more impressive than 18/60.

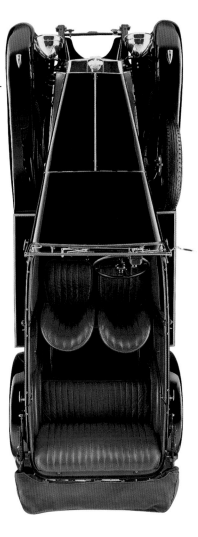

Adjustable dampers

So the driver could tailor the ride and handling to suit himself, the shocks were easily adjusted by compressing the friction plates closer together.

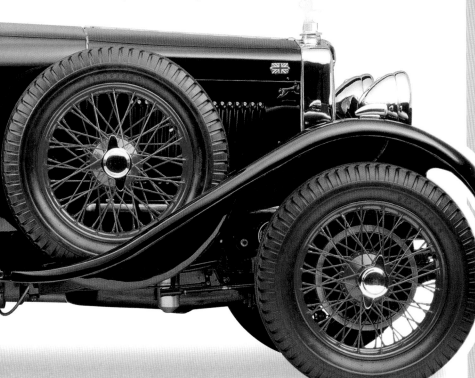

Specifications

1930 MG 18/80 MkI

ENGINE

Type: Inline six cylinder
Construction: Cast-iron block and head
Valve gear: Two valves per cylinder operated by single overhead cam
Bore and stroke: 69.0 mm x 110.0 mm
Displacement: 2,468 cc
Compression ratio: 5.8:1
Induction system: Two sidedraft SU carburetors
Maximum power: 60 bhp at 3,200 rpm
Maximum torque: N/A
Top speed: 80 mph
0-60 mph: 22.8 sec

TRANSMISSION

Three-speed manual

BODY/CHASSIS

Steel ladder frame with wood-framed steel and alloy convertible bodywork

SPECIAL FEATURES

Handling can be tuned to the driver's taste by adjusting the shocks.

The windshield opens at the bottom to provide cooling and ventilation.

RUNNING GEAR

Steering: Worm-and-wheel
Front suspension: Beam axle with semi-elliptic leaf springs and friction shock absorbers
Rear suspension: Live axle with torque tube, semi-elliptic leaf springs and friction shock absorbers
Brakes: Drums, 14 in. dia. front, 14 in. dia. rear, mechanically operated
Wheels: Knock-on/off wire spoke
Tires: 5 x 19 in.

DIMENSIONS

Length: 163.0 in. **Width:** 61.0 in.
Height: 62.5 in. **Wheelbase:** 114.0 in.
Track: 48.0 in. front and rear
Weight: 2,580 lbs.

MG **M-TYPE MIDGET**

The tiny 847-cc Midget marked the birth of the affordable small British sports car. Existing sedan components were used to create a car with great character and, for the day, impressive handling and performance.

"...great road holding."

"The tiny engine is smooth and flexible and makes the lightweight Midget as fast as cars with engines twice the size. The gearshift is easy and the steering incredibly direct and light. The suspension, ride and handling combine to give great road manners for its day. With a car so small, the driver is aware of every movement on the road, allowing instant correction. And yet the ride is comfortable enough to permit long journeys to be undertaken."

The Midget has a simple charm that is reflected in the fascia design.

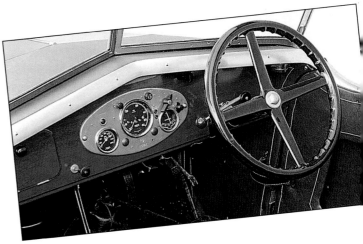

ver the Wolseley company, orris also acquires its powerful all overhead-cam engine.

5 enhanced its reputation th the Midget-engine J2.

)29 Based on the lorris Minor, a small, open-o sports car is released by MG own as the M-Type Midget. e basic car uses a four-cylinder rsion of the Wolseley engine.

e TC established the MG me in the U.S.

931 MG develops e M-Type into the ster C-Type, usually known as e Montlhéry after the famous ench race track. Just 44 of ese are made and they are tremely successful racers. nother development is the nger wheelbase D-type.

932 The M-Type nd its derivatives are scontinued.

UNDER THE SKIN

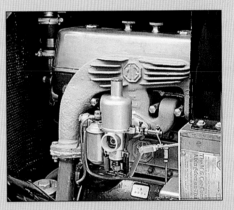

Worm-and-wheel steering

Live rear axle with semi-elliptic leaf springs

Cable-operated drum brakes front and rear

Inline four

Minor changes

MG stands for Morris Garages, so it should be no surprise to learn that the first of the Midgets was little more than a rebodied Morris Minor. The same basic and simple chassis frame was used, carrying the same solid front axle and live rear axle. Both axles are suspended on semi-elliptic leaf springs with friction shocks. The brakes are four-wheel drums, with cable rather than hydraulic actuation. A three-speed manual is the only transmission.

THE POWER PACK

Sophisticated design

Although it is small and has only two main bearings, the M-Type's engine was much more sophisticated than most others its size. What sets it apart is the overhead-cam layout in an era when even a pushrod overhead-valve engine was advanced. It was originally a Wolseley design, which was a factor behind the Morris takeover in 1928. It is all cast-iron, with the usual small bore and long stroke (2.24 inches x 3.27 inches) of the day, but it has alloy pistons and duralumin connecting rods. Because it is only a 847-cc unit, power output is low at 20 bhp, but its design made it very tunable for racing.

Midget racer

More desirable than the standard M-Type is the limited-production C-Type (Montlhéry) model that was developed from it. Particularly sought after are the ones with a Powerplus supercharger. The chassis was improved, and although engine size went down to 746 cc so that it could compete in the 750-cc racing class, it was tuned and performed well. All M-Types are in demand today.

The Midget provided a low-cost entry into open-top motoring.

MG **M-TYPE MIDGET**

The M-Type Midget's lightweight fabric-covered bodywork, with its angled rakish windshield, was designed to make the car look fast and, thanks to its boat-tail rear, quite exotic compared with its rivals.

Overhead-cam engine

The overhead-cam four-cylinder engine is a wonderful design. For the racing version, a new cam was fitted, with different valve timing and stronger valve springs to allow higher engine speeds.

Three-spe
transmissi

Three gears we
considered enough for t
M-Type. First gear takes t
car to 24 mph, second to
mph and top to around
mph, eventually. T
gearshift pattern has f
gear at the bottom le

Gravity fuel feed

The M-Type's tiny engine does not use much gas and easily averages 40 mpg. This is just as well, as it relies on a gravity feed rather than a pump to get gas from the tank to the carburetor. The filler is located under the hood.

Fabric body

One of the keys to the MG's performance was lightness that was helped by the original cars having fabric-covered, ash-framed body panels rather than a sedan body.

Live rear axle

Power is fed through an open driveshaft to the live rear axle. Semi-elliptic leaf springs suspend and locate the axle, and work well, helped by the fact that the MG's track is so small.

Cable brakes

There are drum brakes on all four wheels, and because the MG is so tiny and light, the drums are also very small. To get even moderate braking, the cable system that connects them to the brake pedal has to be in good condition and perfectly adjusted.

Adjustable shocks

The Midget has adjustable shocks for all four wheels. These are of the Hartford friction type, in which the stiffness is adjusted simply by screwing the round friction plates tighter together.

ENGINE
Type: Inline four-cylinder
Construction: Cast-iron block and head
Valve gear: Two valves per cylinder operated by a single overhead camshaft
Bore and stroke: 2.13 in. x 3.27 in.
Displacement: 847 cc
Compression ratio: Not quoted
Induction system: Single carburetor
Maximum power: 20 bhp at 4,000 rpm
Maximum torque: Not quoted
Top speed: 64 mph
0-60 mph: 45.0 sec.

TRANSMISSION
Three-speed manual

BODY/CHASSIS
Separate ladder-type steel frame with fabric-covered two-door convertible body

SPECIAL FEATURES

Protruding from the top of the radiator is an ornate temperature gauge.

The V-angled two-piece windshield looks stylish and sporty.

RUNNING GEAR
Steering: Worm-and-wheel
Front suspension: Beam axle with semi-elliptic leaf springs and friction shock absorbers
Rear suspension: axle with semi-elliptic leaf springs and friction shock absorbers
Brakes: Drums (front and rear)
Wheels: Center-lock wire spoke, 27-in. dia.
Tires: Crossply, 4 x 27

DIMENSIONS
Length: 123.0 in.   **Width:** 50.0 in.
Height: 54.0 in.   **Wheelbase:** 78.0 in.
Track: 41.5 in. (front and rear)
Weight: 1,120 lbs.

MG **TC**

Based on the pre-war MG TA, the TC was a runaway success. Its attractive looks and spritely performance helped it to sell in large numbers here in the U.S.

"...traditional sporty feel."

"Although it's based on standard components from the Morris/Wolseley range, the engine in the MG TC is much more peppy. An improved four-speed transmission gives it sharp acceleration and a traditional sporty feel when shifting through the gears. The engine development lacks the refinement of the chassis which inherits the flexibility of the basic production cars. Stiffer suspension helps to increase stability and allows for more aggressive driving."

With the front windshield folded flat, the TC feels much faster than it actually is.

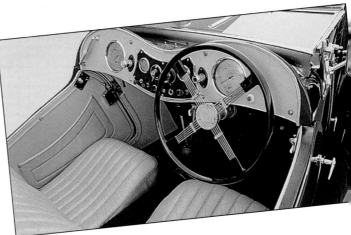

935 MG is taken ver by the Nuffield rganization, parent company Morris/Wolseley.

e-war T-series models used slightly different chassis.

936 The first MG o be designed at the orris plant in Cowley appears. is called the MG TA.

939 The MG TB eplaces the TA. It features new 1,250-cc engine.

945 Following the nd of WWII, roduction of a modified ersion of the TB resumes. amed the TC, it is fitted with pgraded bumpers and lights nd is sold in the U.S.

he last of the legendary -series MGs was the 1953-55 TF.

949 After 10,000 models have been made, roduction of the MG TC comes o an end.

Worm-and-peg steering

Separate steel frame

Four-wheel drum brakes

In-line four

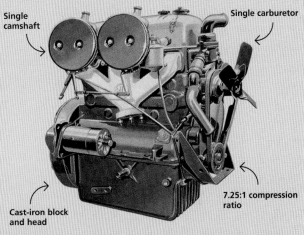

Wider chassis

To the naked eye, the differences between the MG TB and TC are negligible. However, the TC's chassis is 4 inches wider between the rear door pillars. Although it is a small car, this increase provides a roomier feel. Major changes were also made to the suspension. Shackles replaced the sliding trunnions for the road springs and Luvax-Girling shock absorbers were fitted to give the chassis a more responsive feel.

THE POWER PACK

Compact engine

The MG TC inherited the XPAG engine that had been first used in the TB. Based on the 1,140-cc, XPJM engine that was displayed in a Morris Ten at the 1938 Motor Show, the 1,250-cc unit produced 54 bhp at 5,200 rpm and was compact and suitable for tuning. In the TB, the engine was originally mated to a non-synchromesh, four-speed transmission. A more advanced version that offered synchromesh on second and third gears was fitted to the TC.

Single camshaft

Single carburetor

7.25:1 compression ratio

Cast-iron block and head

Rhd only

The TC's success in the U.S. is often credited to GIs who fell in love with the TC while stationed in Europe and bought their own cars when they returned home from the war. Despite the number of cars exported, TCs were made only in right-hand drive form.

TCs helped establish MG as a popular marque in the U.S.

MG TC

In its day, the MG TC was virtually unopposed in its class. Among small sports cars, it had the best combination of classic styling and affordability.

Split-window roof

The convertible top on the TC had a unique split rear window. Its top came in colors that matched the car's trim. They were originally only available in cream, red and green, but other colors were added as the TC grew in popularity.

Folding windshield

All TCs had a standard folding windshield that provided a real wind-in-the-hair driving experience. Those who preferred not to wear goggles were able to keep the windshield in its upright position.

Spare wheel

The spare wheel is mounted on the back of the fuel tank providing convenient access when required. Unlocking the center nut requires a mallet.

Chrome bumpers

No bumpers were fitted to UK-spec TCs, but in order to comply with legislation, U.S. export models had full-width chrome bumpers front and rear.

Single fog light

The single horn and fog light arrangement at the front is characteristic of all early MG T-types.

Rear lights

As well as bumpers, U.S.-spec models have special rear lights that contain built-in turn signals.

Specifications

1949 MG TC

ENGINE

Type: In-line four-cylinder

Construction: Cast-iron block and head

Valve gear: Two overhead valves per cylinder operated by pushrods

Bore and stroke: 2.62 in. x 3.54 in.

Displacement: 1,250 cc

Compression ratio: 7.25:1

Induction system: Single carburetor

Maximum power: 54 bhp at 5,200 rpm

Maximum torque: 64 lb-ft at 2,700 rpm

Top speed: 73 mph

0-60 mph: 21.2 sec.

TRANSMISSION

Four-speed synchromesh

BODY/CHASSIS

Separate steel frame with channel-section main sidemembers and tubular cross-bracing

SPECIAL FEATURES

The spare wheel is mounted on the back of the fuel tank.

All TCs had a windshield that could be folded flat.

RUNNING GEAR

Steering: Worm-and-peg

Front suspension: Beam axle with semi-elliptic leaf springs and lever-arm shock absorbers

Rear suspension: Live axle with semi-elliptic leaf springs and lever-arm shock absorbers

Brakes: Drums, 9-in. dia. (front and rear)

Wheels: Center-lock wire, 19-in. dia.

Tires: Crossply, 4.5 x 19 in.

DIMENSIONS

Length: 144.5 in. **Width:** 56.0 in.

Height: 53.2 in. **Wheelbase:** 94.0 in.

Track: 45.0 in. (front and rear)

Weight: 1,845 lbs.

Morgan SUPER SPORTS

The Morgan was the most popular three-wheeler ever, and was produced for more than 40 years. It served as inexpensive transportation, but people quickly became aware of its performance possibilities: even today, tuned versions can beat four-wheeled cars in vintage racing.

"...a wheel is missing."

"The Morgan's cockpit is very narrow, but you're totally in tune with your surroundings. It's not easy to drive at first, with a hand throttle instead of a foot pedal, wide-spaced gears and high-ratio steering. However, you soon learn to enjoy the acceleration and acquire the art of steering the car on the throttle. It hops and skips over bumpy surfaces and darts quickly around fast corners, but it's surprisingly stable considering that a wheel is missing."

A cramped cockpit and minimal weather protection don't spoil the driving experience.

Milestones

1910 H.F.S. Morgan launches his first JAP-engined three-wheeler.

The earlier three-wheelers had almost no sporty pretensions.

1912 A Morgan wins at the first-ever cyclecar meeting at Brooklands.

1928 The Super Sports model arrives. It has lower bodywork and a rounded tail.

Morgan is better known for its long-lived four-wheeler models.

1935 As Morgan branches out into four-wheelers, it launches the Ford-engined F-Type.

1952 The very last F-Type Morgan is produced as the company devotes its attention to four-wheelers.

UNDER THE SKIN

Sliding-pillar front suspension

Burman steering

Twin-tube chassis

Classic V-twin

Simplicity

Reflecting its original role as a bargain cyclecar, the Morgan is simply engineered but effective. The chassis is a twin-tube arrangement, with one of the tubes acting as an exhaust pipe on early models. At the front end is Morgan's sliding-pillar suspension, which is still used today, and there is a swinging fork and leaf springs at the rear—effectively independent suspension for all three wheels. Power goes through a driveshaft and chain with a three-speed manual transmission.

THE POWER PACK

Brought-in power

Morgan trikes came with a variety of engines over the years, from single-cylinders to flat-fours. The classic powerplant has always been an exposed V-twin engine, the most notable was the JAP. Early engines were air-cooled, later ones water-cooled. The seminal Super Sports most commonly used a V-twin by JAP or Matchless which was used in many motorcycles of the period. Other engine brands that have been used include MAG, Blackburn, Anzani and Precision. From 1935, there was also the option of the Ford Model Y four-cylinder side-valve engine.

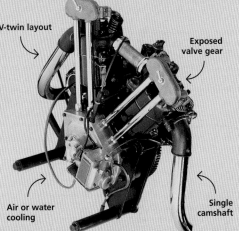

V-twin layout

Exposed valve gear

Air or water cooling

Single camshaft

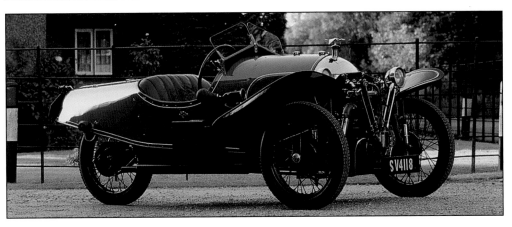

Sport legend

Morgans came in many varieties, from cost-effective runabouts through family transporters to competition racers. The most highly regarded are the Super Sports models, with their low-slung bodies, motorcycle fenders and barrel-back bodywork.

Three-wheeler Morgans have a devoted following.

Morgan **SUPER SPORTS**

Three-wheelers may have begun life as a low priced, simple solution to getting about, but Morgan refined the breed. Some reached speeds as high as 130 mph and became track legends.

Exposed engine

Because of its extreme forward location and a desire for simplicity and easy servicing, the V-twin engine was left completely exposed up front. From the driver's seat you can actually see the valves operating.

Sliding-pillar suspension

Morgans have always been unique with their choice of front suspensions. It is a system of sliding stub axles, first used and patented in 1910 and still produced today at Malvern Link in its four-wheelers. For its day, it was an effective means of achieving independent wheel location.

Curious controls

In terms of its interior design, the Morgan owes more to the veteran era. There are only two pedals, one for the clutch and one for the rear brake. The throttle is applied by a small lever mounted on the steering wheel.

Lever-operated front brakes

The majority of 'ordinary' Morgans had only one brake, a 'band' brake mounted on the rear hub. As an option—but standard on the rapid Super Sports—front drum brakes were fitted. These are operated by cable and handbrake on the outside of the car.

Prop-and-chain drive

Drive is taken from the front engine to the rear wheel initially with a driveshaft to the transmission. Drive then goes to the wheel using a simple chain and sprocket.

Single rear wheel

In terms of stability, a single rear wheel is superior to a single front wheel. Because it has only three wheels, the design is simple (as no differential is necessary) and weight is kept down, allowing the Morgan to perform far better than its modest power output suggests.

Choice of rear-end treatment

Two different rear end styles were offered by Morgan for the Super Sports. The first was a rounded back, but equally popular was the so-called 'barrel back' design.

Specifications

1932 Morgan Super Sports

ENGINE
Type: V-twin
Construction: Cast-iron block and heads
Valve gear: Two valves per cylinder operated by a single camshaft via pushrods and rockers
Bore and stroke: 3.37 in. x 3.37 in.
Displacement: 990 cc
Compression ratio: 7.5:1
Induction system: Single Amal carburetor
Maximum power: 39 bhp at 4,200 rpm
Maximum torque: 50 lb-ft at 2,400 rpm
Top speed: 85 mph
0-60 mph: 14.0 sec.

TRANSMISSION
Three-speed manual

BODY/CHASSIS
Separate thin-tube chassis with doorless steel sports body

SPECIAL FEATURES

The rear body lifts up for easy access to the rear suspension and drivetrain.

The handbrake lever is mounted outside the body.

RUNNING GEAR
Steering: Burman
Front suspension: Sliding stub axles with coil springs and shock absorbers
Rear suspension: Pivoting fork with quarter-elliptic springs and shock absorbers
Brakes: Drums (front and rear)
Wheels: Wire, 18-in. dia.
Tires: 4.00 x 18

DIMENSIONS
Length: 124 in.   **Width:** 59.0 in.
Height: 40.0 in.   **Wheelbase:** 85.0 in.
Track: 49.5 in. (front)
Weight: 954 lbs.

Pontiac **TORPEDO EIGH**

Before World War II, Pontiac was fighting to beat Buick in the intermediately-priced car market. In 1940 the company had a new weapon, the Torpedo, and because of its huge success rate, it was built through 1948.

"...beautifully relaxed."

"Don't underestimate the attractions and abilities of a big, sidevalve, 4.1-liter, straight eight. It revs almost silently, producing 190 lb-ft of torque at a very low rpm that wafts along the massive Custom Torpedo in a beautifully relaxed way. Its weight guarantees an incredibly smooth ride, there's hardly any roll through corners, and the handling characteristics are nearly neutral. The interior and dashboard have typical 1940s styling.

Hand-crafted embellishments give the Pontiac's interior real charm.

1940 Pontiac introduces a new name

to its lineup, the Torpedo or the Series 29. It is only built as a four-door sedan or two-door coupe. Both bodies are new and built on a longer chassis. The head, straight-eight engine has its compression ratio increased to 6.5:1.

The 1934 Pontiac 8 was advanced in using coil-spring suspension.

1941 The Torpedo range is extended with a

wide range of bodies, including a convertible and a six-window, four-door sedan. There is also a sleek fastback body style for the Streamliner Torpedo.

Pontiacs, such as this Chieftain, used straight eights until 1955.

1946 Post-war production continues

with basically the same models as before the war, until more modern styling is introduced in 1949. For 1950, the L-head is stretched and continues until Pontiac's V8 appears for 1955.

UNDER THE SKIN

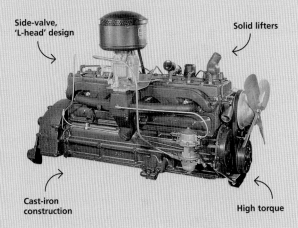

Live rear axle

Independent front suspension

Hydraulic brakes

In-line eight

Long lasting

For 1941, the Torpedo range rode on the longest wheelbase (122 inches) used by Pontiac. As usual, there is a separate chassis frame with few crossmembers but a large central X-brace and two main side rails close together at the rear of the engine and widening out to the rear live axle on semi-elliptic leaf springs. The front suspension is an advanced fully independent system and the brakes are hydraulically-operated, four-wheel drums.

THE POWER PACK

Going straight

Pontiac had yet to enter the V8 age and for the biggest-engined Torpedoes it relied on a straight-eight. It is all cast-iron and uses sidevalves arranged in a line along one side of the engine, making it what's known as an L-head. The valves are opened with solid lifters by a block-mounted camshaft on one side and operate upside down compared to modern overhead-valve engines. By 1941, its dimensions are undersquare with a long stroke for high torque output and 103 bhp at a relaxed 3,500 rpm.

Side-valve, 'L-head' design

Solid lifters

Cast-iron construction

High torque

Super soft top

The most desirable of all the Torpedoes is the two-door convertible. But it's worth considering either of the two coupes in the range, the two-door Business Coupe or two-door Sports Coupe, even if their performance is slightly less impressive.

The Sports Coupe has conservatively sophisticated styling.

Pontiac **TORPEDO EIGHT**

The Custom Torpedo might lack the dramatic flowing lines of the fastback Streamliner Torpedoes but it still showed the way of things to come in body design, marking an end to separate headlights.

In-line eight-cylinder

Sidevalve engines seem very old-fashioned now, particularly in-line, eight-cylinder units, but they did have their advantages. At moderate engine speeds they run very smoothly and with a long stroke produce large amounts of torque.

Sealed beam headlights

In 1940, General Motors pioneered the sealed beam-type headlight in which the glass, reflector and bulb came as one unit and were replaced together instead of changing a separate bulb. They were regarded as a great advancement giving more light than standard headlights during the 1940s.

Integrated headlights

It was only a few years before the Torpedo that Pontiac had separate headlights mounted on the fenders, so the evolution of faired-in headlights built right into the fenders came very quickly.

Separate chassis

The chassis is of the perimeter type with two main outer box-section sidemembers and a central X-brace. The body is held on to the chassis by rubber mounts.

Rectangular grill

The switch to an almost rectangular radiator grill for 1941 was a sign of things to come as the old-fashioned upright grills gave way to lower, wider ones through the 1950s and 1960s.

Live rear axle

Like virtually all contemporary American cars the Torpedo uses a live rear axle. Pontiac gave it a name—'Duflex'—and promoted its telescopic shocks that reduced sway.

Specifications

1941 Pontiac Torpedo Eight

ENGINE

Type: In-line eight-cylinder

Construction: Cast-iron block and head

Valve gear: Two in-line side valves per cylinder operated by a single block-mounted camshaft

Bore and stroke: 3.25 in. x 3.75 in.

Displacement: 249 c.i.

Compression ratio: 6.5:1

Induction system: Single, twin-choke, Carter carburetor

Maximum power: 103 bhp at 3,500 rpm

Maximum torque: 190 lb-ft at 2,000 rpm

Top speed: 88 mph

0-60 mph: 18.9 sec

TRANSMISSION

Three-speed manual

BODY/CHASSIS

Separate box-section steel chassis frame with central X-brace and steel two-door coupe body

SPECIAL FEATURES

Pontiac's distinctive Indian's head mascot adorns the hood of this Torpedo.

Some critics termed the rectangular radiator grill the 'tombstone' grill.

RUNNING GEAR

Steering: Worm-and-sector

Front suspension: Double wishbones with coil springs and telescopic shocks

Rear suspension: Live axle with semi-elliptic leaf springs and telescopic shock absorbers

Brakes: Hydraulically-operated drums

Wheels: Pressed steel disc, 16-in. dia.

Tires: 6.0 x 16

DIMENSIONS

Length: 201.0 in   **Width:** 64.5 in.

Height: 65.0 in.   **Wheelbase:** 122.0 in.

Track: 58.0 in. (front), 61.5 in. (rear)

Weight: 3,325 lbs.

Rolls-Royce SILVER GHOST

For a time, the Silver Ghost truly was the best car in the world for those rich enough to afford Rolls-Royce's supreme craftsmanship, unbeatable reliability and high-class image. In fact, it was so good that it remained in production for nearly 20 years in various forms.

"...total mechanical harmony."

"Although the 75 bhp of the Alpine Eagle-type Silver Ghost doesn't sound like much, it's enough to take it past 80 mph where it can cruise all day. Unlike more modern Rolls-Royces, it's agile too—with just one and a quarter turns of the steering wheel from lock to lock, the Ghost will take even sharp corners with ease. One of the biggest surprises is the effortlessness with which it moves, every part working in total mechanical harmony. The transmission requires practice, but in a Ghost you hardly need to change gears."

Silver coachwork and its whispering quietness gave the Silver Ghost its name.

1906 First 40/50 series cars are unveiled— the 13th example is the original Silver Ghost.

1909 The Ghost's engine is enlarged from 7,036 to 7,428 cc, increasing power output from 48 bhp to 60 bhp.

Silver Ghosts have coachbuilt bodies like this 1910 Roi des Belges.

1911 A special Silver Ghost drives from London to Edinburgh in top gear only with a top speed of 78 mph, resulting in the London-to-Edinburgh model.

1913 Success in the immensely difficult Alpine Trial leads to the sporty, open four-seater Alpine Eagle model.

1918 Following World War I, Silver Ghosts are made under license in Springfield, Illinois.

1923 The Silver Ghost is finally given a brake servo, the type designed and used for years by rivals Hispano-Suiza.

1925 Silver Ghost production ends.

UNDER THE SKIN

Separate channel-section chassis

Coachbuilt bodywork

Straight-six separate from transmission

Leaf sprung beam axle

Refined in-line six

Conservatism

Rolls-Royce was always very conservative and there is certainly nothing radical about the Silver Ghost with its channel-section ladder chassis frame. The four-speed transmission is in the center of the car rather than being in unit with the engine so there can be a very short and precise linkage to the external gear lever mounted outside the driver's door.

THE POWER PACK

Silent luxury

The Rolls-Royce in-line six was built as two groups of three cylinders with each cylinder having dual ignition and two valves in the side of the combustion chamber. Rolls-Royce had already tried overhead valves on previous models, but resorted to side valves because they are quieter and more suitable for such a luxury and high-quality car. The engine was not designed for outright power, but for refinement. There is no head gasket because cylinder head and block are cast in one piece.

Dual ignition

Side valves help reduce mechanical noise

One-piece cylinder heads and blocks

Straight-six built in two blocks of three cylinders

Real Ghost

There is only one real Silver Ghost. The famous all-silver car which still exists was the 13th car in the 40/50 series and built in 1907. Soon people were calling all the 40/50 cars Silver Ghosts—it was never an official model name, but has since become the generic term for this model.

Only the 13th 40/50 built can be described as the real Silver Ghost.

Rolls-Royce **SILVER GHOST**

For a Rolls-Royce, the Silver Ghost was amazingly versatile. It could carry stately formal bodywork in near silence, beat all comers in demanding Alpine Trials competitions and even perform as an armored car in World War I.

Side-valve engine

There are different types of side-valve engines. The Silver Ghost's is an L-head—the valves are along one side of the engine with their heads upward operating in the combustion chambers above them.

Alpine Eagle bodywork

Silver Ghosts carry a diverse range of bodies. This is the open Alpine Eagle style as used in the 1913 Alpine Trial.

Solid axle

Like all cars of its era, the Silver Ghost has a solid front axle. In this case, it is an 'I' section beam mounted on semi-elliptic leaf springs.

Cantilever re spring

Rolls-Royce chang the rear suspensi design several tim settling on a syste of cantilevered ser elliptic rear spring

Alloy pistons

Although heavy iron pistons were common before World War I, Rolls-Royce used lighter alloy pistons, which eased the stress on the crankshaft and its bearings.

Four-speed transmission

The Ghost's engine has a huge torque output, but the Alpine Eagle model has a four-speed transmission. This way, owners would not be embarrassed by steep mountain passes as they could be with the previous three-speed model.

No front brakes

For most of its life, the Silver Ghost had no front brakes, even when some rivals like Hispano-Suiza had switched to four-wheel brakes.

Solid nickel plating

It is no wonder the finish on Rolls-Royces is durable. Nickel plate was applied in thin layers which were soldered to the metal underneath.

Specifications

1913 Rolls-Royce Silver Ghost Alpine Eagle

ENGINE

Type: In-line six-cylinder side-valve
Construction: Cast-iron monoblock with alloy crankcase and pistons
Valve gear: Two side valves per cylinder operated by single gear-driven camshaft
Bore and stroke: 4.49 in. x 4.76 in.
Displacement: 7,428 cc
Compression ratio: 3.5:1
Induction system: Single Rolls-Royce twin-jet carburetor
Maximum power: 75 bhp at 1,800 rpm
Maximum torque: Not quoted
Top speed: 82 mph
0-60 mph: Not quoted

TRANSMISSION

Separate four-speed gearbox

BODY/CHASSIS

Ladder-type steel frame with crossmembers and customer's choice of coachbuilt bodywork

SPECIAL FEATURES

There are two sets of spark plugs. One set runs off a trembler coil system, the other by magneto.

Spirit of Ecstasy mascot was modeled after motoring pioneer Lord Montagu's secretary, Eleanor Thornton.

RUNNING GEAR

Steering: Worm and nut
Front suspension: Beam axle with semi-elliptic leaf springs
Rear suspension: Live axle with cantilevered semi-elliptic leaf springs
Brakes: Rear drums only, rod operated
Wheels: 35-in. wire spoked
Tires: Dunlop grooved square tread beaded edge 895 x 195

DIMENSIONS

Length: 192 in.   **Width:** 162.5 in.
Height: 161 in.   **Wheelbase:** 143.5 in.
Track: 56 in. (front and rear)
Weight: 2,856 lbs. (chassis only)

Rolls-Royce **PHANTOM**

After almost 20 years in production the immortal Silver Ghost, the car Rolls-Royce had called 'the Best Car in the World,' was ready to be replaced. Its worthy replacement was the Phantom I, with an advanced overhead-valve engine.

"...effortless power."

"Not quite as silent as its illustrious predecessor, the Phantom I it makes up for it with effortless pulling power thanks to greater torque. Left in top gear, the Phantom will still accelerate strongly and is totally relaxed cruising at up to 80 mph, which few cars of the day could ever reach. Steering is direct, high-geared and surprisingly light. The ride is superb, but the brakes, despite their servo assistance, are in a different world from today's."

A right-hand gearshift and steering wheel controls ensure the Phantom requires concentration to be driven well.

925 With the 40/50 howing its age, it is time r a new top-of-the-line model. lls-Royce simply modifies the /50 chassis and fits a new, erhead-valve, in-line, six-linder engine to increase wer to 100 bhp. The car is own as the new Phantom.

sing an all-new chassis Phantom were launched in 1929.

926 New Phantom roduction also starts Rolls-Royce's factory in ringfield, Massachusetts. ese cars are left-hand ive and have three-speed ansmissions as standard.

he Phantom III boasted Rolls-oyce's first V12 engine.

929 Replacing the lew Phantom is a lore modern car with an all-new hassis, the Phantom II. The 1926-ntage car is retitled Phantom I.

931 Phantom I roduction carries n in the U.S. until 1,241 ars are built.

Separate channel steel chassis

Leaf springs front and rear

Four-wheel drum brakes

Torquey straight-six

Conservative

Built on a modified version of the previous Silver Ghost chassis, the Phantom's frame is a massive channel steel ladder-type config-uration. Suspension design is equally conservative, with a solid front axle and leaf springs, plus a live rear axle with long cantilever leaf springs to give a comfortable ride. Unlike the early Ghost, there are brakes on all four wheels, with a mechanical servo borrowed from Hispano-Suiza. The transmission is a four-speed manual.

THE POWER PACK

Making the best better

By 1925 Henry Royce felt confident that he had perfected the refinement needed to switch from the sidevalve engine used in the famous Silver Ghost to a more modern and efficient overhead-valve unit. This layout provided increased power and torque. The engine configuration was still an in-line six, effectively with two three-cylinder blocks joined and topped by a detachable head: at first it was made from cast iron, then alloy. At 4.5:1, the compression ratio was low and valve timing mild as the engine relies on its sheer size of 7.7 liters to generate staggering torque at just over 1,000 rpm.

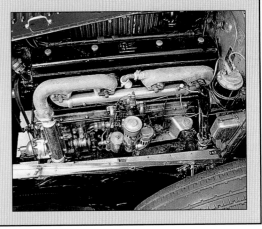

U.S. bodies

The most attractive of the Phantom Is are some of those built in the plant in Massachusetts. Mechanically they are virtually identical, but they, particularly the Brewster-styled bodies, are far more elegant than the British cars.

U.S.-built Phantom Is often had very flamboyant styling.

Rolls-Royce PHANTOM I

The Phantom I chassis could carry a variety of coachbuilt bodies depending on customer requirements. The most attractive of all are those built at the Rolls' factory in Springfield, Massachusetts.

Overhead-valve engine

Based on the 40/50 engine, but with overhead valves, pushrods and a single block-mounted camshaft, the long-stroke, 7.7-liter six boasts phenomenal torque (320 lb-ft) for its day.

Twin ignition system

Because ignition systems were not that reliable in the 1920s, Rolls-Royce used a twin-spark system with two spark plugs for each cylinder; a magneto fired one set and a coil was used for the others. This all changed for the Phantom II. Rolls-Royce felt confident enough to use just one set of plugs.

Solid front axle

Rolls-Royce continued to use a solid front axle with the wheels turning on kingpins. The whole setup is supported and located by semi-elliptic leaf springs.

Nickel plating

To make the finish as durable as possible, Rolls-Royce did not rely on electroplating and chroming but used extremely thin sheets of nickel (0.006 inches thick) which were cut and soldered to the metal.

Drum brakes

It was not until 1924 that Rolls-Royce relied on front brakes. The Phantom I has mechanically operated drums front and rear with a servo driven by the transmission.

Live rear axle

Unlike the Ghost, the Phantom I has cantilever leaf springs for the live axle.

Spirit of Ecstasy

The famous 'Spirit of Ecstasy' radiator mascot was modeled by Charles Sykes.

Specifications

1927 Rolls-Royce Phantom I

ENGINE
Type: In-line six-cylinder

Construction: Cast-iron block and head

Valve gear: Two valves per cylinder operated by a single block-mounted camshaft

Bore and stroke: 4.25 in. x 5.50 in.

Displacement: 7,668 cc

Compression ratio: 4.5:1

Induction system: Single Rolls-Royce twin-jet carburetor

Maximum power: 107 bhp at 2,500 rpm

Maximum torque: 320 lb-ft at 1,200 rpm

Top speed: 80 mph

0-60 mph: 24.0 sec.

TRANSMISSION
Four-speed manual

BODY/CHASSIS
Separate ladder-type channel section chassis with customer's choice of bodywork

SPECIAL FEATURES

A spotlight carried on the A-pillar was to help the driver read signs at night.

There was ample storage space in the Phantom's capacious trunk.

RUNNING GEAR
Steering: Worm-and-nut

Front suspension: Solid axle with semi-elliptic leaf springs and friction shock absorbers

Rear suspension: Live axle with cantilever leaf springs and friction shock absorbers

Brakes: Drums (front and rear)

Wheels: Wire spoke, 21-in. dia.

Tires: 7.00 x 21

DIMENSIONS
Length: 190.3 in.   **Width:** 72.0 in.

Height: 60.0 in.   **Wheelbase:** 143.3 in.

Track: 57.0 in. (front), 56.0 (rear)

Weight: 4,725 lbs.

Rolls-Royce **PHANTOM III**

The Phantom III was the last car on which Henry Royce worked. When its production came to an end, much of Royce's design philosophy went with it. The era of producing cars with a seeming disregard for development costs was over.

"...utmost smoothness."

"You know this is a special car as soon as you get in. Even if you've been in a modern Rolls, you'll be shocked by the craftsmanship. The engine is special, too. Rolls-Royce's attention to detail in matching the weights of reciprocating parts results in considerable performance being delivered with the utmost smoothness. The independent front end and the sheer weight of the car result in a refined ride, but enthusiastic cornering isn't what this car's about."

The craftsmanship inside the Phantom has to be seen and felt to be believed.

Milestones

1925 Rolls-Royce launches the New Phantom. Running alongside the existing Twenty model, it has a new bi-bloc engine and four-wheel brakes. It is built both in Britain and at the U.S. Rolls-Royce factory in Springfield, Massachusetts.

The Phantom I was built in Britain and the U.S.

1929 The Phantom II replaces the New Phantom, although the Springfield factory continues to build the New Phantom, now known as the Phantom I.

The improved Phantom II was introduced in 1929.

1935 The Phantom III uses a new V12 engine, replacing the old car's straight-six. It also has independent front suspension.

1939 The war brings production to an end after 717 Phantom IIIs have been built.

Non-unit engine and transmission

Live rear axle

Independent front suspension

Chassis advances

The Phantom III used a hefty steel chassis with a live rear axle suspended on semi-elliptic leaf springs like its predecessor. The advances came at the front end. It was the first Rolls-Royce to use an independent front suspension. It was based on a General Motors-derived coil- and-wishbone design by Maurice Olley, a former Rolls-Royce engineer. Brakes are four-wheel drums with Rolls-Royce's own mechanical brake booster.

Alloy V12

THE POWER PACK

Aeronautical engine

To compete with the V12s of Cadillac, Lincoln and Packard, Rolls-Royce designed its own new unit for the Phantom III. The company had previous experience with V12s in its airplane engine business, and the new engine had block and heads cast in Hiduminium, an alloy developed for this work and produced by High Duty Alloys (hence its name). Wet cylinder liners were employed, and the overhead valves were actuated with pushrods by a central camshaft that, as on every Rolls-Royce engine since 1904, was gear- rather than chain-driven. All rotating parts were meticulously balanced.

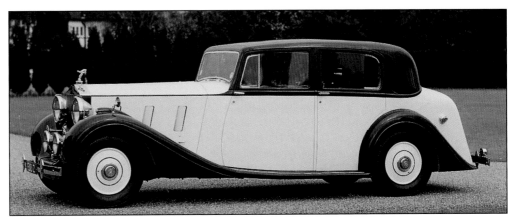

Landmark

The Phantom III is a real landmark Rolls-Royce. Not only were its V12 and independent front suspension new to the company, but it was also the last car that Henry Royce worked on. He died at age 70, a year into its development.

The Phantom III is the last of the great pre-war Rolls-Royces.

Rolls-Royce **PHANTOM III**

When you bought a Phantom III, you bought a bare chassis and then chose a coachbuilder to body it. This particular car carries a Henri Binder body and was built for the 1936 Paris Motor Show.

Separate transmission

The four-speed manual transmission has a right-hand gearshift, but the actual transmission is mounted separate from the engine. A short driveshaft connects it to the engine

Front suspension

The Phantom III was the first Rolls-Royce to have independent front suspension. It is a coil-and-wishbone setup derived from a General Motors design.

Wire wheels

The Phantom III actually uses wire wheels. They are hidden behind these painted wheel discs. This was common practice in the 1930s.

Strong chassis

Unlike previous models, the Phantom III was offered in only one chassis length. It was a strong box-section frame with a bolt-on central cruciform section for extra rigidity.

...lloy V12 engine

...he V12's block and heads were cast from ...iduminium, an aluminum alloy developed ...y Rolls-Royce for its airplane engines.

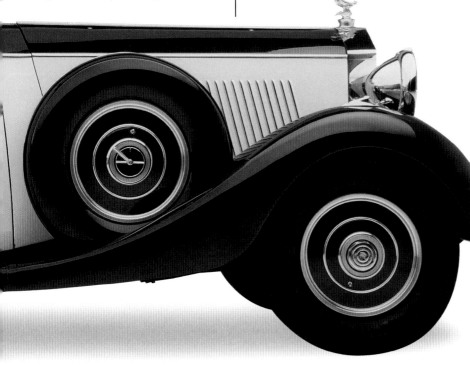

Specifications

1936 Rolls-Royce Phantom III

ENGINE
Type: V12
Construction: Alloy block and heads
Valve gear: Two valves per cylinder operated by a single camshaft via pushrods and rockers
Bore and stroke: 3.25 in. x 4.50 in.
Displacement: 7,340 cc
Compression ratio: 6.0:1
Induction system: Single Stromberg carburetor
Maximum power: 160 bhp at 4,000 rpm
Maximum torque: Not quoted
Top speed: 93 mph
0-60 mph: 16.5 sec.

TRANSMISSION
Four-speed manual

BODY/CHASSIS
Steel chassis with four-door body

SPECIAL FEATURES

Enormous headlights dominate the front end of the Phantom.

This Binder-bodied Phantom III has thin side-mounted spare wheels.

RUNNING GEAR
Steering: Worm-and-sector
Front suspension: Wishbones with coil springs and lever-arm shock absorbers
Rear suspension: Live axle with semi-elliptic leaf springs and lever-arm shock absorbers
Brakes: Drums (front and rear)
Wheels: Wire, 18-in. dia.
Tires: 7.00 x 18

DIMENSIONS
Length: 205.0 in. **Width:** 83.5 in.
Height: 69.0 in.   **Wheelbase:** 142.0 in.
Track: 60.3 in (front), 61.0 in. (rear)
Weight: 5,800 lbs.

Stutz **BEARCAT**

Developed from an Indianapolis 500 racing car, the Stutz Bearcat has style and charisma but most of all, a huge engine that could take it far beyond the performance of most cars on the roads in the U.S.

"...antique supercar of its time."

"A maximum of 60 bhp doesn't sound like much to get excited about, but the Stutz's big 390-cubic inch four has an enormous amount of torque. Like its maximum power, it seems to be produced right off-idle. The hefty bellowing Bearcat, with its barn-like aerodynamics, could turn a top speed of 80 mph, making it an antique supercar of its time. It'll cruise effortlessly at 60 mph and the sensation of speed is something even a Ferrari driver would be impressed by. It's surprisingly easy to drive, too: the controls are light and the gearshift simple."

It doesn't come more basic than this. Stutz drivers have a bare minimum of instruments and controls.

Milestones

1911 Harry Clayton Stutz builds a car for the first Indianapolis 500. It finishes 11th out of a field of 44 and inspires Stutz to start production.

1915 the Stutz White Squadron team dominated racing in the U.S.

1912 Stutz begins to build six- and four-cylinder cars.

1914 A Stutz car finishes fifth in the Indy 500.

1915 Erwin 'Cannonball' Baker breaks the U.S. coast-to-coast record driving a Bearcat over 3,700 miles at an average speed of 13.7 mph. It sounds slow, but there were no proper roads across the country at this time.

Later Stutz cars were more civilized than the Bearcat, but still offered good performance.

1916 Stutz introduces its own 360-cubic inch 'T' head engine giving a top speed of 71 mph. Production continues into the 1930s progressing into a more civilized car.

UNDER THE SKIN

Rear transaxle

Monocle windshield

Engine is load bearing

Ladder-type chassis

Huge straight-four

Beefy Bearcat

There is one novelty to the Bearcat's large, robust, ladder-type chassis. In a foretaste of modern racing car design, the engine acts as part of the chassis. Another unusual feature of the overall design is having the three-speed transmission in unit with the final drive and mounted at the rear, where it helps weight distribution, off-setting the bulk of the huge Wisconsin four-cylinder engine at the front. The standard wheels are wooden spoke; wire wheels were only an option.

THE POWER PACK

'T' head

Stutz bought its engine from the Wisconsin company. It is a large four-cylinder 'T' head side-valve design, so called because the valves are below the cylinder head working up into the combustion chambers, with the intake manifold on one side, and the exhaust manifold on the other. The engine itself is made up of two cast-iron blocks of two cylinders each, mounted on an alloy crankcase. Two plugs per cylinder are used and it produces its maximum power at a very low 1,500 rpm.

Two plugs per cylinder

Side-mounted camshafts

Cast-iron block

Alloy crankcase

Stutz racer

The Bearcat was a direct development of the Stutz racing car that finished in 11th position in the first Indy 500 in 1911. The production car's minimal bodywork reflects its racing origins. Bearcats used the same 'T' head engines as the original racer.

Stutz racer developed into the Bearcat.

Stutz BEARCAT

Before World War I, both Stutz and Mercer defined their American sports cars—the Bearcat and the Raceabout—as big, brash and fast.

'T' head Wisconsin engine

All Bearcats were built with a Wisconsin 'T' head in-line four. It's much bigger than the side-valve four used in the Mercer Raceabout but only fractionally more powerful.

Bucket seats

Bucket seats were developed to keep the occupants from falling out of the car since it didn't have any doors.

Twin spark ignition

With large cylinders there's an advantage in two spark plugs per cylinder, but they are there for reliability and not to improve the efficiency of the engine.

High ground clearance

With tall wheels and the semi-elliptic leaf springs mounted on top of the axles, the Bearcat has a lot of ground clearance, keeping the transaxle far above the road.

Optional wire wheels

Standard equipment for the Bearcat was wooden wheels with detachable rims. Lightweight wire-spoke wheels, such as these, were optional.

Rear transaxle

Harry Clayton Stutz saw the advantage of mounting the transmission to the rear along with the transaxle to improve weight distribution.

Shift and handbrake levers

In the early days of motoring there was no place for the gearshifter inside the cockpit. It stayed outside, in this case mounted alongside the handbrake lever.

Advance/retard mechanism

The driver adjusted the engine timing with a control on the steering wheel. The ignition could be advanced as the engine speed rose.

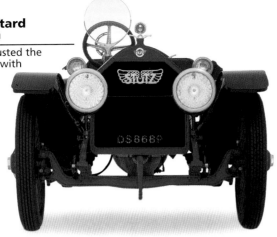

Rear drum brakes

As usual with pre-World War I cars, there are brakes on the rear wheels only, although there is a manual handbrake also acting on the rear wheels.

Specifications
1914 Stutz Bearcat

ENGINE

Type: Wisconsin four-cylinder side valve
Construction: Alloy crankcase with two cast-iron blocks and alloy pistons
Valve gear: Two side valves per cylinder operated by side-mounted camshafts on either side of the block
Bore and stroke: 4.76 in. x 5.51 in.
Displacement: 390 c.i.
Compression ratio: 4.0:1
Induction system: Single updraft Stromberg HA carburetor
Maximum power: 60 bhp at 1,500 rpm
Maximum torque: Not quoted
Top speed: 80 mph
0-60 mph: Not quoted

TRANSMISSION

Rear-mounted three-speed manual

BODY/CHASSIS

Steel ladder frame chassis with the engine acting as stressed chassis member. Open speedster-type bodywork

SPECIAL FEATURES

The monocle windshield gave the driver protection from the slipstream.

A radiator-mounted 'Boyce Motometer' is used to monitor water temperature.

RUNNING GEAR

Steering: Worm-and-nut
Front suspension: Beam axle with semi-elliptic leafs and friction shocks
Rear suspension: Live axle with semi-elliptic leafs and friction shocks
Brakes: Rear drums only, 16 in. dia.
Wheels: Wire spoke, 4.5 in. x 34 in.
Tires: 4.5 in. x 34 in.

DIMENSIONS

Length: 160 in. **Width:** 65.9 in.
Height: 63.4 in. **Wheelbase:** 120 in.
Track: 55.9 in. (front and rear)
Weight: 2,500 lbs.

Sunbeam 3-LITRE

One of the great sports tourers of the 1920s, the Sunbeam 3-Litre used a sophisticated twin-cam, six-cylinder engine developed from Grand Prix racing to give it performance that hardly any other car could touch.

"...comfortable ride."

"Cars from the 1920s usually require a lot of effort to drive. However, the Sunbeam has a rewarding engine that cries out to be revved and is helped by a slick gearshift that enables a skillful driver to move through the transmission even though there's no synchromesh. Heavy at first, the steering soon lightens up at speed and is very precise. The long wheelbase gives a comfortable ride, while the four-wheel brakes give the confidence to exploit the performance."

The sporty nature of the 3-Litre is shown in the multigauge dashboard.

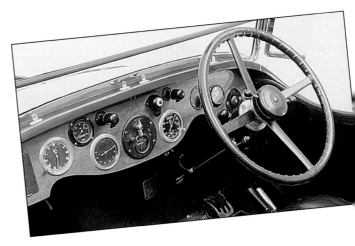

1924 Sunbeam

...oduces a prototype 3-Litre.

...unbeam's glory years were the ...920s, when its racing cars were ...rand prix contenders.

1925 After some

...echanical revisions, ...e 3-Litre goes into production ...small numbers. At Le Mans, ...e of the two-car team ...nishes second.

...ggest of the 1931 Sunbeams, ...as the stately Twenty-Five.

1926 To overcome

...he stress of Le Mans, ...stronger car, known as the ...sanction, is built. Engine ...oling is improved, as is the ...linder head design. This year, ...0 3-Liters are made.

1929 Adding a

...upercharger increases ...ower to 135 bhp. Production ...nds this year after 315 cars have ...een made in total. Later models ...ave a plunger-type central ...assis lubrication.

UNDER THE SKIN

Semi-elliptic leaf-sprung rear suspension

Friction shocks front and rear

Solid front axle

Race-derived straight-six

Long and thin

The Sunbeam's long wheelbase and narrow track were different from those of its rivals. Its two main chassis rails are joined by crossmembers that hold the engine in line with the transmission, plus its solid front axle, which is suspended on semi-elliptic leaf springs. The rear suspension consists of a live axle on long, cantilevered, semi-elliptic leaf springs, and there are friction shock absorbers front and rear. A more modern feature is the very effective brakes on all four wheels.

THE POWER PACK

High-revving racer

Based on the racing straight-eight, 3-liter, twin-cam engine from Sunbeam's early-1920s Grand Prix cars, the 3-Litre's engine differed in having a cast-iron monobloc, with the block and head in one casting, to eliminate head gasket problems. It is a long-stroke design, though less so than most engines at the time, and consequently revs higher. At 6.4:1 the compression ratio was higher than most, and there are two angled valves per cylinder in almost hemispherical combustion chambers, worked by two gear driven overhead camshafts. The maximum power of 90 bhp is produced at 3,800 rpm.

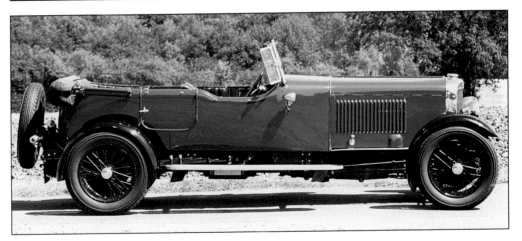

Super-rare

Easily the fastest of the Sunbeam 3-Litres was the rare supercharged model, which has an increased power output of 135 bhp. It cost a little more than the regular models, but failed to win a major race. Only one survives.

A supercharged version became available in 1929.

Sunbeam 3-LITRE

It was long, upright, and narrow, but the odd looks of the Super Sports should not fool you; this is a car built by engineers right at the forefront of car design who knew what it took to win on the race track.

Twin-cam engine

Some elements of the 3-liter, inline six-cylinder, twin-cam engine are contemporary, such as angled valves in hemispherical combustion chambers. Other elements, like having the block and head cast as one, show its age.

Four-wheel brakes

One feature that made the 3-Litre stand out was the brakes. There are extremely effective drums on all four wheels, which was uncommon during the 1920s.

Cycle fende

Unusually narro cycle-type fende are fitted, whi move with the fro wheels. They a more firmly attach than is typical fo car of this era, with substantial b running to t brake carri

Cantilever rear springs

Most cars in the 1920s had their live rear axles held on semi-elliptic leaf springs with the axle in the center of the springs. On the Sunbeam, the springs were ahead of the axle line so the axle was cantilevered.

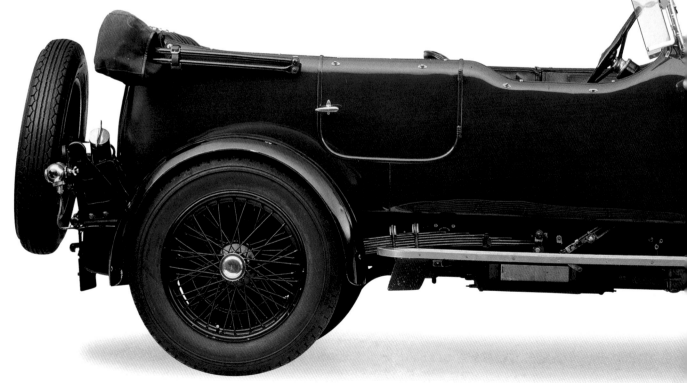

Different bodywork

This body is the classic 3-Litre tourer, but the car could have any one of a number of different bodystyles made by outside coachbuilders; some had formal upright sedan bodies and some had Weymann fabric on wooden-frame bodywork.

Specifications

1926 Sunbeam 3-Litre

ENGINE
Type: Inline six-cylinder
Construction: Cast-iron monobloc
Valve gear: Two valves per cylinder operated by two gear-driven overhead camshafts
Bore and stroke: 3.0 in. x 4.4 in.
Displacement: 2,916 cc
Compression ratio: 6.4:1
Induction system: Two Claudel Hobson H42A carburetors
Maximum power: 90 bhp at 3,800 rpm
Maximum torque: Not quoted
Top speed: 95 mph
0-60 mph: N/A

TRANSMISSION
Four-speed manual

BODY/CHASSIS
Separate channel-section ladder frame with customer choice of bodywork

SPECIAL FEATURES

The rear lights on the 3-Litre are tiny by today's standards.

The car came complete with a fully equipped tool kit.

RUNNING GEAR
Steering: Screw-and-nut
Front suspension: Beam axle with semi-elliptic leaf springs and Hartford adjustable friction shock absorbers
Rear suspension: Live axle with torque tube, cantilever springs and Hartford adjustable friction shock absorbers
Brakes: Drums (front and rear)
Wheels: Center-lock wire spoke
Tires: Beaded edge, 120 x 820 mm

DIMENSIONS
Length: 188.0 in.   **Width:** 67.0 in.
Height: 71.4 in.   **Wheelbase:** 130.5 in.
Track: 55.0 in. (front and rear)
Weight: 2,688 lbs.

Swallow Sidecar **SS100**

Before the Swallow Sidecar Company changed its name to Jaguar they had already built the car that started the Jaguar sports car tradition. This ancestor of the E-type was stylish, fast and yet cheaper than its rivals.

"...strictly a two-seater."

"The SS100 is nothing but a cramped two-seater. The driver is wedged behind the large steering wheel—which you have to hold close to the chest—and the gear lever is almost hidden under the dashboard, where you can easily grab the handbrake by mistake. But the joy of driving the SS makes you soon forget the cramped interior. The ride is stiff and, like most pre-war sports cars, it's not happy on bumpy roads. The engine, particularly the larger, 3¹/₂-liter version will cruise effortlessly at 93 mph."

The six fascia dials, from left, were for water, battery, fuel, rpm, oil and mph.

**935 In March SS
nows** the SS90, a sports car
at looks very similar to the
100, which follows. It is based
a cut-down sedan SS1 chassis
th a 2,663-cc side-valve engine
oduced by Standard Motor
. and modified by SS. In
ptember the SS100 appears.
has a purpose-built chassis,
d- rather than cable-operated
akes and an overhead-valve
rsion of the Standard engine.

*e 1939 3½-liter SS100—
aised for effortlessness.*

**936 An SS100
riven by journalist**
mmy Wisdom completes the
pine Rally with no penalty
ints at all. Another car wins
e Marne GP.

**938 SS enlarges the
ngine** size to 3,485 cc and
e 3½-liter car is sold alongside
e 2½-liter model. The bigger
ngine increases top speed and
ops the 0-60 mph figure by a
uple of seconds. Also in this
ar, the single SS100 coupe is
uilt for the London Motor Show.

**939 Production
eases** after 314 cars have
een built; 198 2½-liter models
nd 116 3½-liter cars.

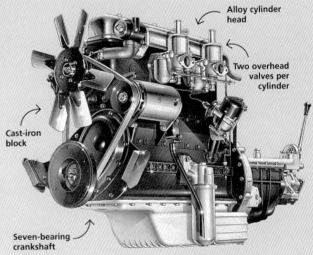

Pressed-steel
ladder chassis

Solid front axle

Leaf springs
front and rear

In-line six cylinder

Good tradition

Mechanically there was
nothing revolutionary about
the SS100. The chassis is a
traditional pressed-steel
ladder frame with a
center X brace
for stiffness. When
opposition like BMW's 328
had independent front
suspension, the SS100 still
had a solid front axle with
leaf springs. Traditional it
may have been, but it all
worked very well.

THE POWER PACK

Advanced motor

The engine is more impressive
than the chassis. It was SS's first
overhead-valve design with the
alloy cylinder head designed by
the famous tuner Harry
Weslake. The bottom end is still
basically the cast-iron block from
the Standard side-valve engine
used before, but Jaguar added
an improved seven-bearing
crankshaft and better
lubrication. It is a long-stroke
design giving lots of torque. The
engine was enlarged to 3,485 cc
in 1938 and power went up
from 104 bhp to 125 bhp.

Alloy cylinder
head

Two overhead
valves per
cylinder

Cast-iron
block

Seven-bearing
crankshaft

Single coupe

All SS100s are convertibles, except one. A single, streamlined coupe
was built for the London Motor Show in 1938. It was intended for
production in 2½- and 3½-liter forms but the war interrupted Jaguar's
plans. The car survives in the hands of a private collector.

*The SS100 coupe was
priced at $795
depending on engine
size.*

Swallow Sidecar **SS100**

The founder of Swallow Sidecar (which later became Jaguar), William Lyons, knew what made a desirable sports car. Apart from performance it had to have a long hood and low roof—a theme later repeated with the E-type.

Solid front axle

Although other cars had independent front suspension, the SS100 made do with a solid axle underslung below the chassis rails.

Six-cylinder engine

SS started by having its engines made for it by another, larger, manufacturer, the Standard Motor Co. By the time of the SS100 the six-cylinder engine had been considerably modified by SS, to give 104 bhp and later 125 bhp.

Four-speed transmission

No pre-war cars had more than four gears. The SS did have the advantage of synchromesh on the three top gears, although first is a 'crash' gear.

No trunk

The stylish shape of the SS100 meant there was no room for a trunk. Luggage had to be carried on the shelf behind the front seats.

Finned alloy oil pan

To help cool the engine the oil pan is alloy rather than steel, with fins to help to dissipate the heat.

Rear-hinged doors

Before the war, rear-hinged doors were the fashion, but they weren't very safe since they could fly completely open, particularly in open-bodied cars that flexed.

Finned brake drums

The brake drums on the SS100 were finned to prevent them from overheating under heavy or continuous braking.

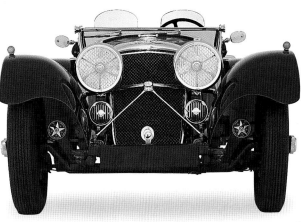

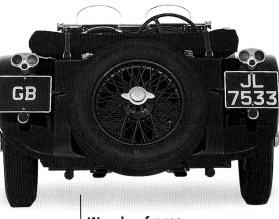

Windshield

If the windshield was folded down the driver would use the small aero-shield, which in theory made the car more aerodynamic.

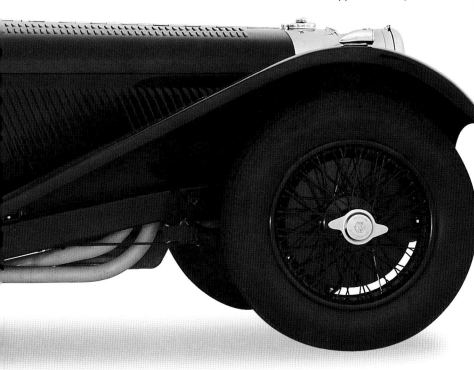

Wooden frame

The alloy and steel body panels are mounted on a wooden ash frame, which is made of a number of parts glued and screwed together. Morgan uses a similar approach today.

Specifications
1937 Jaguar SS100

ENGINE

Type: Straight-six overhead valve
Construction: Cast-iron block and alloy head
Valve gear: Two valves per cylinder operated by single block-mounted camshafts
Bore and stroke: 2.87 in. x 4.17 in.
Displacement: 2,663 cc
Compression ratio: 7.0:1
Induction system: Two SU carburetors
Maximum power: 104 bhp at 4,500 rpm
Top speed: 95 mph
0-60 mph: 13.8 sec.

TRANSMISSION

Four-speed manual

BODY/CHASSIS

Two-seater sports car body on pressed-steel ladder chassis

SPECIAL FEATURES

Although almost obsolete, friction shocks were retained at the front to help out the hydraulic ones at the rear.

By simply turning this knob, the windshield can be folded flat to minimize wind resistance.

RUNNING GEAR

Steering: Worm-and-nut
Front suspension: Beam axle with semi-elliptic leaf springs, friction and hydraulic shocks
Rear suspension: Live axle with semi-elliptic leaf springs and hydraulic shocks
Brakes: Drums all around, rod operated
Wheels: 18-in. dia. Dunlop center lock wire wheels
Tires: Dunlop Sport 5.25 in. x 18 in.

DIMENSIONS

Length: 152.9 in.
Width: 62.9 in.
Height: 50 in.
Wheelbase: 104 in.
Track: 54 in. (front and rear)
Weight: 2,575 lbs.

Talbot-Lago **T150-SS**

This SS or Super Sports version of the Talbot-Lago T150 was the very top of the range, produced in tiny numbers at an outrageous price, and powered by a hemi-head 4-liter straight-six engine.

"...outstanding acceleration."

"You feel buried in the claustrophobic SS, but it's worth it for the view of the long hood and sensuously sculpted fenders. Although the straight six is highly tuned, it is still tractable, and the pre-selector transmission works well once you've adjusted to the idea of selecting a gear before you need it. Acceleration was outstanding for the day. Thanks to its independent front suspension, the SS handles superbly."

Simple inside by modern standards, the SS was very luxurious in its day.

Milestones

1935 Major Anthony Lago takes over the French company automobiles Talbot.

Figoni and Falaschi also designed convertible SS model.

1936 The first collaboration between Talbot-Lago and Figoni & Falaschi appears at the Paris Motor Show. It features a spectacular two-door coupe with a 4-liter straight-six engine.

The very last of the Talbot-Lago line was the America/Simca.

1937 Figoni and Falaschi body a Talbot-Lago especially for an American bobsled racer named McEvoy. So aerodynamic is the car that it is driven 600 miles from Paris to Cannes on ordinary roads, averaging almost 70 mph. Eight more cars are soon built and given the name Goutte d'Eau (teardrop).

UNDER THE SKIN

X-braced separate chassis

Independent front suspension

Four-wheel drum brakes

Hemi straight six

More strength

Strong U-shaped rails were connected by round-tube crossmembers and a massive X-brace to form an extremely strong structure. It carried a traditional live axle at the rear mounted on semi-elliptic leaf springs with friction shocks. The front suspension was more advanced, though, with a lower transverse semi-elliptic leaf spring along with independent control arms.

THE POWER PACK

Hemi development

The big straight-six found in the 150-SS was more than just a stretched development of the existing Talbot-Lago engine. Its crankshaft was better supported on seven (rather than four) main bearings, and the cast-iron block was also bored out to 3.60 inches from 3.12 inches, although the stroke was unchanged. Head design was advanced for the time, with two valves per cylinder operated by a single high block-mounted camshaft with pushrods and rockers. This design allowed an efficient crossflow head, fed by three carburetors.

Work of art

One of the most elegant automobiles ever built, the Figoni & Falaschi-designed SS was a perfect example of outrageous conspicuous consumption, only affordable by the extremely wealthy. They have long been considered a near-priceless commodity.

Only nine Goutte d'Eau coupes were ever built.

Talbot-Lago **T150-SS**

'Goutte d'Eau' translates as 'teardrop,' after the aerodynamic theories of the 1930s. Not only was it one of the outstandingly beautiful shapes made before the war, it was efficient, too—these sleek coupes could reach 115 mph.

Straight-six engine

With its hemi head, the Talbot-Lago straight-six had great tuning potential. Its good gas flow was properly exploited by having three carburetors, and with different cam timing and higher compression ratios, it could be tuned to deliver as much as 180 bhp.

Suicide doors

Suicide doors were still common in the 1930s despite the safety hazard they presented. They also seem ideally mated to the flowing lines of the SS and are in keeping with the art deco excess.

Drum brakes

Talbot-Lago had a very impressive competition record with cars mechanically similar to the SS models. This showed in their brakes, huge 14-inch-diameter drums that virtually filled the space right up to the wheel rims. They were also finned to dissipate heat and avoid fade: this was vital in the SS models, as the wheels were so shrouded by the fenders.

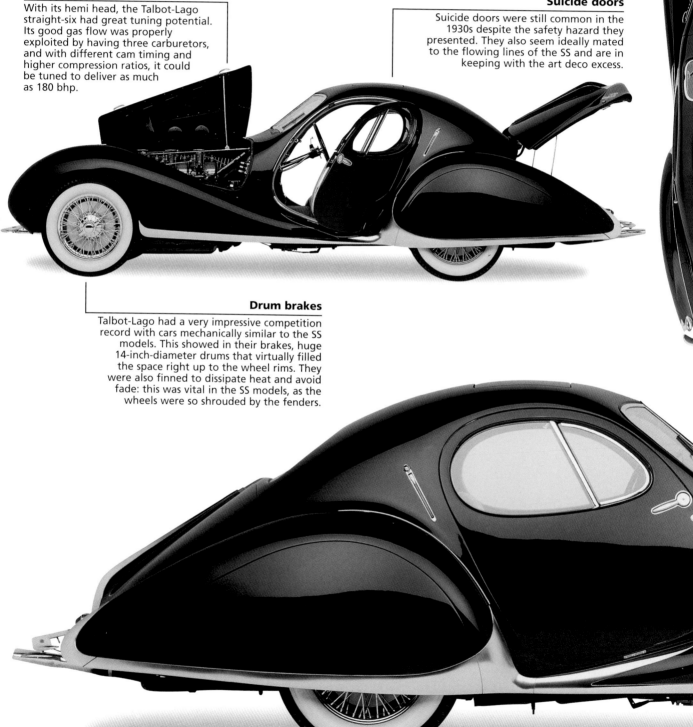

Specifications

1937 Talbot-Lago T150-SS

ENGINE

Type: Inline six cylinder

Construction: Cast-iron block and alloy head

Valve gear: Two valves per cylinder operated by single block-mounted camshaft with pushrods and rockers

Bore and stroke: 3.60 in. x 4.18 in.

Displacement: 3,996 cc

Compression ratio: 8.0:1

Induction system: Three downdraft Solex carburetors

Maximum power: 140 bhp at 4,000 rpm

Maximum torque: N/A

Top speed: 115 mph

0-60 mph: 11.5 sec

TRANSMISSION

Four-speed Wilson pre-selector

BODY/CHASSIS

Separate steel frame with steel two-door coupe bodywork

Pre-selector transmission

Talbot-Lago owner Anthony Lago had bought the rights to the Wilson pre-selector gearbox in 1928. It became a fitment on Talbot-Lagos. The driver would select the next gear he wanted with a small lever and then simply press the shift pedal.

Separate chassis

There were many similarities between the straight-six Delahaye 135 and the Talbot-Lago 150-SS, as both shared the X-braced chassis and suspension.

SPECIAL FEATURES

Semaphore turn signals retracted into the body behind the doors.

A thoughtful touch was the inclusion of an extra set of spark plugs.

RUNNING GEAR

Steering: Worm-and-nut

Front suspension: Leading arms with lower transverse semi-elliptic leaf spring and De Ram friction shock absorbers

Rear suspension: Live axle with semi-elliptic leaf springs and De Ram friction shock absorbers

Brakes: Drums front and rear, 14-in. dia., mechanically operated

Wheels: Armstrong-Whitworth wire spoke, 17-in. dia.

Tires: 6.00 x 17

Live rear axle

Although Talbot-Lago knew the benefits of independent front suspension, it retained a live axle on the rear of the T150-SS, suspended by semi-elliptic leaf springs.

DIMENSIONS

Length: 178.2 in.　　**Width:** 70.5 in.

Height: 56.6 in.　　**Wheelbase:** 104.0 in.

Track: 54.0 in. front, 57.5 in. rear

Weight: 3,310 lbs.

Voisin **C27 FIGONI**

Gabriel Voisin gained fame and fortune building war planes in World War I and then made some of the most unusual and innovative cars ever seen. One of the rarest was the C27—just two were built.

"...totally unique."

"This C27 was designed for those demanding something unique. It's an experience to be savored, from the elegant Figoni bodywork to the superb interior. The sleeve-valve six is quiet and refined and, once you've got some revs on it, it pulls smoothly and powerfully to its 4,000-rpm peak. Voisin gave the C27 stiffer-than-normal springs and its handling matches some contemporary sports cars, but it works best as a fast grand tourer."

Supremely elegant, the C27 boasts only the finest hand-stitched leather inside.

1934 Following its display at the Madrid Auto Salon, Voisin chassis 52001 is purchased by the Shah of Persia and later sold on to the Persian attaché. Gnome Rhône took Voisin over in 1938.

Gabriel Voisin (right) was an engineer of remarkable talent.

1948 The sole surviving C27 is sold on to Monsieur Poirer, who keeps it until the early 1960s. The car is then sold to historian Serge Pozzoli, but it soon changes hands again and ends up neglected in a French barn.

Voisin was most famous for its pusher-type aircraft, this is an A5 B2.

1984 The C27 is finally restored by Claude Figoni, son of stylist Joseph, and Henry Barnard, the son of Voisin's chief engineer. It is later bought by LA collector Peter Mullin and re-restored.

UNDER THE SKIN

Tubular-steel chassis

Servo-assisted brakes

Adjustable shock absorbers

Playing it safe

Surprisingly, in view of how differently he did everything else, Gabriel Voisin kept a traditional separate chassis frame for his cars in the 1930s, although the tubular-steel structure is well stiffened with box-section crossbraces. The suspension it carries is similarly conservative, with a solid forged-beam front axle and a live rear axle, both carried and located by semi-elliptic leaf springs.

Smooth, sleeve-valve six

THE POWER PACK

Sleeve-valve engine

Like all Voisins, the C27 uses a sleeve-valve engine, a design invented by Charles Knight in 1905 and used by Daimler and Mercedes. Instead of conventional valves and camshafts, the intake and exhaust ports are covered and uncovered by the action of cast-iron sleeves around the cylinders. The sleeves are moved up and down by an eccentric shaft acting like a camshaft. The advantages are quiet running and a good pentroof-type combustion chamber shape, but maintenance is awkward and frequent and engine speeds are restricted. That, in turn, restricts power and torque.

Sole survivor

The Figoni-bodied cabriolet (chassis 52001) is now the only surviving C27. It currently resides in Los Angeles and is significant, not only in terms of styling and engineering, but also as a Pebble Beach concourse show-winner.

This Figoni cabriolet has been restored twice so far.

Voisin C27 FIGONI

This open convertible Voisin was one of the more restrained designs by Italian-born Joseph Figoni, who went on to gain even more prestige as part of the great Paris-based styling partnership of Figoni & Falaschi.

Sleeve-valve engine

Voisin used sleeve-valve engines in four-, six- and even 12-cylinder forms. The one in the C27 is a long-stroke, 3-liter, six-cylinder version. The sleeve-valve arrangement gives the cylinder head a more efficient crossflow design.

Dynastart

Instead of having a separate starter motor and dynamo or magneto like other cars, the C27 has a combined system called a Dynastart. One disadvantage is that it weighs 80 lbs.

Nut-and-screw steering

Voisin knew the advantage of high-geared steering. The nut-and-screw system was set up that way because he regarded the price of heavy steering at slow and parking speeds a reasonable price to pay for precision.